HARVEST
and other plays

PRAIRIE PLAY SERIES no.28

For Steve
Thank you so
much for the inspiration
and Comraderi.

Ken Cameron

KEN CAMERON

HARVEST

AND

other plays

edited with an introduction by Anne Nothof
series editor: Diane Bessai

NeWest Press

COPYRIGHT © KEN CAMERON 2010

Library and Archives Canada Cataloguing in Publication

Cameron, Ken, 1969 –
Harvest and other plays / Ken Cameron.

Contents: My One and Only — Harvest — My Morocco.
ISBN 978-1-897126-67-7

    I. Title.

PS8605.A482H37 2010   c812'.6   C2010-902805-8

Series Editor: Diane Bessai
Editor for the Board: Anne Nothof
Author photo: Sean Dennie
Proofreading: Paul Matwychuk

 Canada Council for the Arts   Conseil des Arts du Canada   Canadian Heritage   Patrimoine canadien   Alberta Foundation for the Arts   edmonton arts council

NeWest Press acknowledges the support of the Canada Council for the Arts, the Alberta Foundation for the Arts, and the Edmonton Arts Council for our publishing program. We acknowledge the financial support of the Government of Canada through the Canada Book Fund for our publishing activities.

NEWEST PRESS

#201, 8540–109 Street
Edmonton, Alberta T6G 1E6
780.432.9427
www.newestpress.com

No bison were harmed in the making of this book.
printed and bound in Canada   1 2 3 4 5 13 12 11 10

INTRODUCTION

Ken Cameron's Multiple Metatheatrical Stories

Storytelling is at the heart of Ken Cameron's plays. They may vary radically in style, form, and content, but they all connect directly and personally with the audience through narrative disclosure. The stories are typically about families — their misunderstandings and miscommunications, their attempts to connect or disconnect, their functions and dysfunctions. In *Harvest*, a retired farming couple tells the story about the considerable consequences of renting out their home, and in the process enact a marital interrelationship both wrinkled and burnished by time. In *My Morocco*, the story of the death of a sister becomes a means of reconnecting with family across great separations of time and space. In *My One and Only*, the young protagonist graphically recalls his relationships with Marilyn Monroe and with his mother, in a time warp which demonstrates that stories inform the present as well as the past. Each story responds to loss — of a home, a sister, a lover.

The style and structure of each play are determined by the content. Like his early mentor, Sharon Pollock, Cameron continually experiments with dramatic form to suit the story. Form determines perspective, time sequence, and tone, enabling ironic juxtapositions and surprising narrative shifts. *Harvest* is a two-hander in which the protagonists play many roles to create a community. *My Morocco* is an introspective monologue which conjures an exotic locale for an expression of personal grief. *My One and Only* is a memory play, the characters summoned from the past through recollection. His plays are about the ways in which plays are constructed, and he resists the formula of a "well-made-play."

While pursuing his education — first a Bachelor of Arts degree at McGill University and later a Master of Fine Arts degree at the University of Calgary — Cameron studied a variety of critical theories and aesthetics, which opened up many possibilities for dramatic storytelling. His views on theatre as a collaborative process are informed by his exposure to reception theory, which posits that meaning is constructed by the reader or audience, rather than being inherent in the text: signification materializes only in the act of reading or, in the case of theatre, in the act of viewing and listening in a shared experience. Dialogue is a series of cues to the audience, inviting a construction of meaning.

The influence of reception theory is also evident in the construction of the three plays in this collection: each one explores the ways in which meaning is constructed — through language, memory, role-playing. For Ken Cameron, the "meaning" of his plays is determined not by the playwright alone, but through a collaborative process of author, director, actors, and audience. What the director and actors choose to do with the text may be complementary or subversive. To this end, Cameron provides very little in the way of stage directions, which may attempt to control the reception of the play; in fact, he wrote two early plays entirely without stage directions, believing that the dialogue should be self-sufficient. From the words of the story, actors construct performance. However, although he is frustrated by playwrights who refuse to make changes to their sacred text, and has frequently revised his own scripts, Cameron does draw the line at production changes which may distort the story; radical revisions should be done only in consultation with the playwright.

From working with the multidisciplinary One Yellow Rabbit Performance Theatre in Calgary, Cameron learned the value of collective creation, and although he directed his own earlier plays for ten years, he now prefers to work with a director who can make stylistic choices which may open up the text to alternative readings while providing a coherent perspective. Although he was initially determined to produce and direct *My One and Only* himself, Ron Jenkins, the artistic director of Workshop West Theatre, and Vanessa

Porteous, dramaturg at Alberta Theatre Projects, persuaded him to accept an offer to premiere the play at ATP's playRites Festival, where it was directed by Gail Hanrahan, and later at Workshop West Theatre, where it was directed by Ron Jenkins. Conversely, Cameron enjoys working as a director and dramaturg with other playwrights. He has played many roles in Canadian theatre.

Cameron observes that the Canadian theatre industry is currently undergoing a shift from the privileging of text towards a collective involvement as a generational phenomenon. Many new works evolve through a series of readings and workshops to which dramaturges, actors, and directors contribute. He believes the new play workshop process in Canada to be more deeply collaborative then other Western English-language theatres: in Britain, too much reverence for the playwright may lead to overlong and static productions; while in the United States, too much focus on the star power of an actor can sometimes put pressure on playwrights to reshape their scripts for the wrong reasons. He sees Canadian theatre as more a director's theatre, where the editorial function of the dramaturg is given prominence in new play development. To illustrate his point, he notes that most of the larger regional theatres in Canada are under the creative control of directors who are not playwrights, with important exceptions such as Peter Hinton, the Artistic Director of English Theatre, and Wajdi Mouawad, Artistic Director of French Theatre, both at the National Arts Centre in Ottawa. Even playwright development centres, once the bastion of playwrights, are increasingly managed by dramaturg/directors.

This scenario isn't necessarily negative in Cameron's eyes, since he himself grew up in a "post-dramaturgical era": his second play, *Mrs. Talleyhouse,* was workshopped at Playwrights Workshop Montreal in 1992 while he was still defining himself as a playwright. As he puts it, "I have never known anything *but* the new play development workshop. For me, a play comes into its own with the collaborative input of a director, dramaturg and actors; while I feel the playwright should always have the final word about what goes into his or her play, insisting solely on the primacy of one person's vision and rejecting input from colleagues does not, as far as I am concerned, lead to good playwriting."

The development history of the plays in this volume bear this out: *My One and Only* was workshopped at the Springboards new play festival in Edmonton and again workshopped two years in a row at the Banff Playwrights Centre with then-ATP Artistic Director Bob White, Ron Jenkins, and Vanessa Porteous, finally seeing more than forty drafts. *My Morocco* was shaped and honed with input from director Andy Curtis, assistant director Dan Perry, and Ken's wife Rita Bozi (who is also one of the characters in the play), while Cameron rehearsed the role on his feet. The expansion of *Harvest* into a two-act play was done through a series of workshops at The Ship's Company and Alberta Playwrights Network with key input from a variety of actors, director Ian Prinsloo and artistic director of the Blyth Festival, Eric Coates.

Cameron's undertaking of the role of artistic director of the Magnetic North Theatre Festival since 2008 is further testimony to his belief in theatre as collaborative and inclusive, and a demonstration of his hope that the playwright have a stronger voice at the national level. The Magnetic North Theatre Festival annually alternates between Ottawa and another Canadian city — so far, the event has been staged in Edmonton, St. John's, Vancouver, and Kitchener-Waterloo. Cameron notes with surprise that even though he is a playwright, the productions he has programmed at the festival tend more often to be ones which have been created in a collaborative manner rather than individually scripted works requiring the involvement of local actors and directors.

As a playwright, Cameron is sometimes concerned that the modern theatre is witnessing the death (or at least the decline) of the playwright as the primary impetus of play-creation. But he also recognizes that the entire theatre ecology is slowly changing, leaving behind the notion of the playwright who writes a script in isolation and only later requires actors and a director once the work is complete.

On the other hand, that the three plays in this collection are primarily his own creations testifies to the fact that in Canada, the playwright is alive and well. And in the case of *My Morocco*, the playwright is also the performer, telling his own story. Cameron does not see this monologue as entirely his prerogative, however, and in fact in its original ten-minute incarnation at Vancouver's Solo Collective Theatre's monologue festival, it was performed by another actor. Cameron welcomes the involvement of other performers with the published version, and hopes they will create something that he would never be able to imagine.

All of Cameron's plays have an autobiographical element, and he believes this to be true of any art form:

> We often hear writers talk about how art is a conversation between writer and reader, but I think that's incorrect. It seems more accurate to say that the making of art is a conversation with oneself; an attempt to reconcile the disparate aspects of one's own personality in a public forum. At its best, art-making is a constant process of self-regard and public excoriation — a kind of public meditation. This is often mistaken for egotism or self-absorption, and I'm the first to admit that it can often be just that. However, it's surely worth the risk; in order to have anything worthwhile to communicate about the human condition, a frank and honest look at oneself is necessary. (from V. Tony Hauser, *Stage Presence*, 2010)

But his stories also speak to the experiences of others, and he achieves some distance from his source material by approaching it as fiction in order not to be bound by literal facts and to make the plays more dramatically engaging. For example, in *My Morocco*, the actual events took place over two and a half years, which he condensed to one week. *Harvest*, although based on Cameron's parents' experience of relocating and renting, opens up the particular circumstances to consider the anxieties of retirement and letting go of the past. *My One and Only* was triggered by an article in *Saturday Night* about the filming of *River of No Return* in Banff and, like his protagonist, Cameron found the prospect of spending time with the goddess of beauty, Marilyn Monroe, irresistible. Inspired by the Paul Quarrington's novel *Civilization* and Kurt Vonnegut's *Slaughterhouse-Five,* he was also looking for a vehicle for a nonlinear play in which the past would collide with the present.

Harvest began as a one-act play commissioned by Lunchbox Theatre in Calgary. Cameron wanted to develop the play into a two-act version, and even though director Ian Prinsloo was concerned that expanding the work might merely result in the inclusion of extraneous padding, he undertook the job. Prinsloo suggested devoting Act I to Allan and Charlotte's story and Act II to Ron's story, but eventually both playwright and director decided that the primary perspective should remain that of the retired couple.

The result has been a popular success: *Harvest* has been produced many times since its premiere as a full-length work at the Blyth Festival in southern Ontario, and has played in theatres from Sackville, New Brunswick to Edmonton, Alberta, and notably in the playhouse with which Cameron's parents and sister have been involved — the Port Stanley Festival Theatre in Ontario.

The play effectively uses economy of scale — two actors play all the roles, changing roles and genders in an instant and making minimal use of props. This approach presents a challenge to even the most versatile comic performers, but it vividly underscores the fact that Charlotte and Allan are enacting their own story for an audience and trying to understand what happened to them. In the Blyth production, for instance, when Larry Yachimec dangled a variety of hats from the end of a fishing rod to portray the women in the community, the audience response was enthusiastically jubilant. For Cameron, this scene enacts the point in the play in which the whole community becomes fully engaged in the lives of two of its inhabitants — a truly metatheatrical moment in which the audience watches two performers performing characters who are themselves enacting roles. Cameron considers this opportunity for a wider community portrait, which shows the consequences of the depopulation of a small town, the most important result of the enlargement of the play from the original one-act version.

Harvest is also about older people who have spent a life-time together, and know each other's limitations very well, but can still draw strength from each other. As Cameron has observed, the older demographic of summer theatre audiences has been particularly receptive. He was influenced in his choice of older characters by the positive reception of Doug Curtis's play *Mesa,* which portrays a journey of mutual disconnection and discovery from Alberta to Arizona undertaken by a 35-year-old aspiring artist and his 93-year-old grandfather-in-law, a long-retired bank manager. Curtis plays off their divergent philosophies of life against each other, showing both their inadequacies and their strengths. Cameron speculates that his play also owes its success to its broad appeal: older audience members are engaged by seeing themselves portrayed onstage not as stereotypes, but as vibrant, active, complex characters, while younger audience members might be more attracted to the grow-op scenario. Regardless of the topic, however, for Cameron, connection with the audience should be the primary point of theatre.

The audience appeal of *Harvest*'s virtuosic, improvisational role-playing is also characteristic of the monologue form. Although Cameron admits that an advantage of the mono-logue is its cheaper production costs, he also argues that this form offers an opportunity for audiences to experience the ways in which one actor can populate a stage with a wide range of characters and events. He speculates that the mono-logue is more popular in Canada than in the U.S. and Europe because of the exposure afforded by Fringe festivals across the country, which have contributed to the development of an appreciation for the versatility and intimacy of the form.

Indeed, *My Morocco* enjoyed sold-out houses during its tour of the Fringe circuit in 2006. The play is Cameron's attempt to come to terms with the death of his sister, structured as a variation of a travelogue and memoir which gradually assumes the aspects of a nightmare. The playwright begins to construct a play as he tells the story of his sister's illness and death, even imagining how it could be produced, and at the same time realizing that he is exploiting life to make theatre. His meta-theatrical exercise enacts the past in the present, and brings the present back to the past, which finally remains only as an ephemeral voice message on a telephone.

In *My One and Only*, the dilemma faced by the protagonist, Scout, is that he cannot escape the past: "The past didn't go anywhere," he says, and he in effect relives it over and over again, as if in a purgatorial state. This theme asserts itself most spectacularly in the late scene entitled "Sometimes Back," in which the policeman opens the trunk of the car — a Pandora's box stuffed with memories — and time reverses itself as events replay themselves backwards in a stunning metatheatrical moment which demonstrates the simultaneity of present and past. Like the other two plays in this collection, *My One and Only* is also about family: Scout's obsession with Marilyn Monroe is inextricably bound up with his relationship with his mother, for whom he also provides an essential conduit to memory-obliterating liquor, and in terms of whose sexuality he learns to become a man.

For Cameron, what theatre does best is bring a community of people together in one room in order to have a dialogue. The best plays are less like film, and more like a live experience. Theatre also works best when it is conscious of its status as theatre, and when the audience is aware of the play as a construct, and of themselves as participants in the theatrical experience. The three plays in this collection have a common purpose: to connect with an audience, and bring a community together through sharing lived experiences — playing patterns of life through entertaining stories. Publication provides a "living document" of a play, which connects it to a history of performance and to current events — a way of "getting it out there."

Anne Nothof
Athabasca University, 2010

photo of Glenn Nelson
and Coralie Cairns as
Allan and Charlotte by
Walter Tychnowicz

HARVEST

a play in two acts

For Mom and Dad...

PLAYWRIGHT'S INTRODUCTION

It's true: *Harvest* is based on a real story. My parents really did
rent the farmhouse I grew up in to a man who claimed to be
an airline pilot and who used my childhood home to grow
marijuana. They really did nearly lose everything and narrowly
escape by the skin of their teeth.

And when all of this happened, I knew immediately that
I would write a play about it.

I knew this instinctively. Not just because it was clear that
this was a great story which would allow me to explore the consequences of the depopulation of Canada's rural roots and the
growing influence of Canada's drug gangs upon people who
never suspected they'd be entwined in their nets. But because
I knew in my heart that my parents are great characters, and
that their relationship was one that I wanted to capture onstage.

I remember my parents fighting between themselves when
I was young; voices raised in the hall decrying unpaid bills, feet
clomping to the bedroom, a suitcase pulled out from the deep
recesses of the closet, myself cowering under the covers. Today
I am confident that their marriage was no more rocky at the
time than anyone else's, but as a young boy the loud voices left
me terrified that they would divorce, for I knew from television
that such things happened.

Later, after my older sister married, I left home for boarding
school when I was still a teen, returning home only intermit-
tently. I realize now that my parents must have been confronted
with "empty nest syndrome" at what was for them an uncomfortably early age. Over the subsequent years, I watched my parents
"reboot" their relationship, and I swear to this day that during
those periods when the farmhouse groaned in emptiness, they
fell in love all over again. When it came time to write *Harvest*,
I realized that the play I wanted to write had, at its heart, the
rediscovery of their deep, abiding love for each other. The fact

that this happened in the crucible of a crisis was one of my few fictional additions to the real-life incidents.

My parents became theatre people almost by default. They were dubious when I decided to pursue theatre in university, mollified only by wise advice from my art teacher who told them "all honest work is honourable." Once it was clear that I was committed, they were too: driving eight hours from London, Ontario to McGill University in Montreal to see the plays I performed or directed; sometimes hosting late-night cast parties in my small apartment; and never failing to bring homemade pie and maple syrup, which I proudly shared. When I stood in front of an audience of students for my final directing project and asked if we could hold the house for fifteen minutes because my parents had been delayed in a snowstorm, I suspect it was the years of goodwill pies and cookies that ensured an easy agreement amongst my peers.

But my sister told me that she has never seen my parents so enthusiastic as when I returned from university to the local Port Stanley Festival Theatre (with a very urban production of Christopher Durang's *Laughing Wild*) because it was then that they were able to connect what I was doing with their community and their friends. Within a few years, my mother Carolyn had joined the board, eventually becoming board president and being instrumental in the purchase of the building; my father Allister became chair of the building committee at about the same time and put in countless volunteer hours with a hammer and saw; and my sister Beth Evans served a number of years as administrator. They all eventually drifted away from serving the theatre, but for years we were a theatre family.

Carolyn became quite famous for delivering vast quantities of cookies, butter tarts, and pies to the cast and crew backstage, recognizing that these young people (for everyone is "young people" to her, no matter their biological age) were working for a pittance. It's those butter tarts that inspired the scene where Allan and Charlotte debate about delivering furniture and a casserole to Ron.

But my mother's butter tarts also epitomize what is special about small communities: friendliness towards everyone who walks in the door, neighbourliness that knows no municipal boundaries, and conscientiously building a sense of community through gestures both large and small. These values are epitomized in the later scenes of *Harvest*, when both Charlotte and Allan forgive their adversaries for their actions.

My mother is fond of saying that I captured my father perfectly in the character of Allan, but that she is "nothing like that woman onstage." [1] As proof of this, she points to the scene in Tim Hortons, proclaiming that she would never have let Ron off the hook. When the two-act production premiered at the Blyth Festival, a mere hour-and-a-half drive from their home, more than two hundred of their friends saw the play over three weeks. On a lark, my mother distributed surveys, asking her friends if they thought the portrayal was accurate. One of the final questions on my mother's survey was "Would you have let the drug dealer go"?

It's true that this is one of the few scenes in the play that did not happen in real life. In reality, they never did see the tenant again, though my father swears he saw the man leaving a gas station in London just as he was arriving.

The genesis of that scene, like so much in this play, lies with director Ian Prinsloo. A year after the premiere of the one-act version at Calgary's Lunchbox Theatre, during a developmental workshop of the two-act version, Ian pointed to the importance of church in Charlotte's life. Up to this point, the church ladies had represented *community* to me and little more; Ian asked what would happen if Charlotte actually acted upon Christian principles of forgiveness. This is something that so many of us who espouse religion or ethics neglect to do.

---

1 She also claims never to have said, "Lord love a duck" in her life. But when pressed, she will confess that once, while driving a friend to a convention in Toronto a few months after seeing the play, she heard the phrase come out of her mouth ... and nearly drove into the ditch in shock.

And this is where I disagree with my parents' interpretation of themselves. I have observed Allister and Carolyn Cameron for forty years, and I have watched them grow from farmers who were born into a Depression-era world without electricity into cosmopolitan globetrotters who see theatre across the country. I have watched them grow from a young farm couple who had their share of disputes into a loving, generous, and supportive relationship. But I have *never* known them to stray from the small-town values of inclusion and forgiveness that made them the compelling people I wanted to write about.

Allister and Carolyn Cameron, this play is for you.

ACKNOWLEDGMENTS

These thanks must be reproduced in the program of any production of the play:

This play is dedicated to the most wonderful and understanding parents in the world, Allister and Carolyn Cameron.

A one-act version of *Harvest* was commissioned by Calgary's Lunchbox Theatre for their Stage One Petro-Canada Plays series and premiered at Lunchbox in March 2007.

The play received the Enbridge playRites award in 2007 which, in conjunction with the Canada Council for the Arts and the Alberta Foundation for the Arts, funded a workshop at Ship's Company in Parrsboro, Nova Scotia. The play was further developed in a workshop with the Alberta Playwrights' Network (which receives funding support from Theatre Alberta) in partnership with The Blyth Festival. The two-act version of the play premiered at The Blyth Festival in 2008.

Ken Cameron is a member of the Playwrights Guild of Canada.

Special thanks to: Ian Prinsloo, Johanne Deleeuw, Natascha Girgis, Brian Dooley, Elinor Holt, Peter Strand Rumpel, Doug McKeag, Playwrights Theatre Centre, Martin Kinch, Pamela Halstead and Ship's Company Theatre, Eric Coates, The Blyth Festival, and especially Rita Bozi.

PERFORMANCES

A one-act version of *Harvest* was commissioned by Calgary's Lunchbox Theatre for their Stage One Petro-Canada Plays series and premiered at Lunchbox in March 2007.

CAST
Allan: Peter Strand Rumpel
Charlotte: Elinor Holt

PRODUCTION
Director: Ian Prinsloo
Set and Lighting Designer: Terry Gunvordahl
Costume Designer: Jen Gareau
Stage Manager: Marcie Januska
Production Manager: Caitlin Ferguson
House Technician: Jason Pouliot

The two-act version of the play premiered at The Blyth Festival in June 2008.

CAST
Allan: Larry Yachimec
Charlotte: Marion Day

PRODUCTION
Director: Ian Prinsloo
Set and Costume Designer: Shawn Kerwin
Lighting Designer: Bonnie Beecher
Sound Designer: Todd Charlton
Stage Manager: Joanna Barrotta
Assistant Stage Manager: Dini Conte

STAGING

Harvest has been written for a cast of two actors, who will play all of the parts, from the sixty-five-year-old retired farm couple to the thirty-year-old sly criminal to the forty-year-old talkative policeman. They will play these roles without regard for gender or age, and without time-consuming costume changes. The transformation from one character to another will be effected quickly and easily, through voice, mannerism, physicality, the magic of theatre ... and perhaps with the aid of the odd hat.

The characters sometimes address the audience directly using common storytelling conventions, and sometimes erect the fourth wall so they can lose themselves in the scene. Sometimes they use both these conventions at once. In these latter instances, for the sake of clarity, I have tried to use the term "aside" to indicate when they are speaking to the audience and not another character.

The play takes place at the raspberry patch — or perhaps in the middle of a field — across the road from the farm. Here the characters tell us the story of what happened to them. Using simple props and the power of the audience's imagination, they recreate their adventures and all of the necessary locations. It's likely that we don't see the farm which lies offstage, so that their descriptions of it become all the more evocative.

The set might contain a few elements that give a flavour of rural life. One might imagine a wooden apple crate, a battered stepladder, some length of rope, a mailbox, a gravel road. In any case, anything that is placed onstage ought to be used as a prop, costume, or set piece in constructing the scenes.

Like most farmers, both Allan and Charlotte are busy types. They are likely doing something with their hands all the time, even when they are telling the story, be it setting up for the next scene, changing out of some small costume element, packing away a prop or just picking raspberries. This is a useful actor's tool that can help to de-emphasize lines that might otherwise be treated as overly important. Allan and Charlotte have been married for forty-two years, and so even the most significant moments can be played against text — that is to say, treated lightly and "thrown away."

Lastly, it is worth remembering that *Harvest* is, at its heart, a love story. Unable to let go of the past, Allan and Charlotte get themselves into trouble; in the crucible of that experience their love is forged anew.

A NOTE ON PUNCTUATION

When an ellipsis "..." appears in the middle of a line, it usually means a slight pause or groping for thought. However, an ellipsis *before* the line usually means that the character is lying.

A NOTE ON SETTING

The text references many small towns and locations throughout southern Alberta, but I insist that any production should contextualize the play by substituting names of nearby local towns.

HARVEST

ACT ONE

Allan begins the play pacing. He is nervous and anxious, like someone waiting for news which he is certain is going to be very, very bad. He keeps glancing offstage left, into the distance. Allan stops, sighs, and looks down at the ground. He looks up and squints out at the audience.

Allan: Look out there. The fields and fields of crops, swaying in the gentle summer breeze. The row of trees hugging the crick, another line of trees here, making a natural wind-break for the house. The acre and a half of lawn, carved out of what used to be the old apple orchard. This farm is in my blood. I was born on this farm —

Charlotte shouts from stage left.

Charlotte: You were born in a hospital.

Allan: *Ignoring her.* — and I've lived my whole life on this farm.

Charlotte: We lived in the city for five years when were first married.

Allan: *Ignoring her.* This farm has been in my family for one hundred and thirty-eight years.

Charlotte: Your father *bought* it.

Allan: From his cousin.

Charlotte: His fifty-second cousin twice removed.

Allan: Still his cousin.

Charlotte: Who he'd never even met.

Allan: Dang it, Mother, I'm trying to tell a story here.

Charlotte emerges from stage left with a heavy box.

Charlotte: Well, at least get the darn story straight.

Allan: Any sign of him?

Charlotte: Nothing.

Allan: Maybe I should go see what he's up to.

Charlotte: You're not going in there.

Allan: I've already been in there once.

Charlotte: Just … tell the story.

Allan: *Pouting.* I don't remember where I was.

Charlotte: Sure you do.

Allan: No, I don't.

Charlotte: *To the audience.* The farm belonged to Allan's father
who bought it in 1937. He sold the apple orchard to us
in sixty-nine for a dollar. When Allan's father died in
Seventy-one —

Allan: Seventy.

Charlotte: Seventy-one. Allan's mother stayed on the farm
until last year —

Allan: She lived here until she was ninety-one.

Charlotte: Grandma had a stroke while Allan and I were away
for the afternoon. Right here in the raspberry patch.

*The following flashback is performed without too much fanfare or set-up.
Allan crosses the raspberry patch. He stops, startled by something he sees
in between the rows. He squats and checks for a pulse. Charlotte enters.*

Well, she's not in the house — or in the garden — so —

Charlotte stops. Pause.

Should I call someone?

Allan: There's no one to call. It's done.

Charlotte: Oh. Allan, I'm so sorry.

*Charlotte starts to cry. Allan comforts her. Lights return us to the present.
Allan and Charlotte turn to the audience.*

We never should have left her alone.

Allan: It was only for the afternoon.

Charlotte: No one to keep her comfortable except the dog.
Barney wouldn't leave her. Curled up right next to
Grandma, trying to keep her warm.

Allan: Lucky we weren't gone longer. The dog might have had
to eat her to survive.

Charlotte: Allan! Don't joke. One of us should have stayed.
I didn't need —

Allan: Charlotte. We were only gone for a few hours. For forty-
two years you treated that woman like she was your own
mother. Without us she would have gone into the old
folks' home long ago.

Charlotte: If she'd been in a home, there would have been
a nurse by her side in minutes.

Allan: We don't know that. *To the audience:* We didn't decide
right then —

Charlotte: I did.

Allan: — but that was the start of it. If there's one thing I've
learned in forty-two years of marriage it's that trying to
argue when this woman gets an idea into her head is like
trying to talk sense into a tornado.

Charlotte: I swore that I wasn't going to finish out my days
lying flat on my back in the middle of the country where
no one could find me. I made Allan promise that we'd
retire, sell the farm, and move to the city.

Allan: The boy wasn't going to take over the farm, that's for
darn sure. Never showed one bit of interest in farming.
When he was a kid I bought him one of those little toy
tractors from the John Deere dealership, with a little toy
plow and a little toy cultivator.

Charlotte: He never played with them more than once.

Allan: *Bitterly.* Put his damned *Star Wars* figures in the driver's seat. Said he was "terraforming the surface of Mars."

Charlotte: So, there was nothing for it but to put up the For Sale sign.

Allan: Trouble was, we didn't exactly get a lot of offers.

*Charlotte becomes **Istvan**, a seventy-year-old farmer. You would think that, since he emigrated from Hungary after the revolution back in 1956, Istvan would have learned not to butcher the language by now; but you'd be wrong.*

Istvan: What's wrong with it?

Allan: With what?

Istvan: The farm? If you sell it, there must be something wrong with it.

Allan: There's nothing wrong with it, Istvan.

Istvan: Bad drainage? Soil erosioning? Sour gas well?

Allan: No.

Istvan: Rats! You have the rats!

Allan: There is nothing wrong with the farm. I just want to … retire.

Istvan: Retire? Retire! Let me be telling you. I was coming to this country fifty-one years ago —

Allan: I'm your neighbour, remember?

Istvan: — after the revolution —

Allan: I know when you moved here.

Istvan: They chased me out with guns — pow, pow. Retire! A children you was.

Allan: I'm sixty-five, Istvan.

Istvan: See? A children!

Allan: The wife is tired of worrying about the weather every time she goes shopping.

Istvan: Wife! Who listens to wife?

Allan: We want to do some traveling. See the world.

Istvan: For this, we have the TV.

Allan: And the boy isn't going to take over.

Istvan: *Appalled.* No! Your son ...? not ...? A son must wear the father's feet.

Allan: He's not the farming type.

Istvan: *Appalled.* No!

Allan: He lives in the city. You know that.

Istvan: My friend. Such tragedy.

Allan: It's fine. He's got his own thing. With the ... technology ... and the ... cellphone ... He's good at it.

Istvan: He doesn't work.

Allan: He works. With the ... thing. Charlotte explains it better than I do.

Istvan: But not with his hands.

Allan: He works with his head. In an office. In the city. It's the way of the future.

Istvan: But you. Stay young.

Allan: I'm tired, Istvan. I've tried everything. Cows. Pigs. Sheep. Remember the llamas? I've mortgaged this farm and paid it off more times than Elizabeth Taylor's gotten married. I'm lucky I didn't lose it in the eighties. My father never got that close, not once, not even in the Depression.

Pause.

Istvan: I'll be buying.

Allan: What?

Istvan: Farm. I'll be buying.

Allan: You've already got your farm. And you just bought
McKeller's last year. That's a lot of land for someone
who's seventy-five.

Istvan: My boy, Pishta, he helps. Five hundred.

Allan: We're asking seven-fifty.[1]

Istvan: Seven-fifty? With rats, you charge seven-fifty?

Allan: There's no rats.

Istvan: Six.

Allan: The house alone is worth at least two hundred.

Istvan: I have house. Just farm. Six.

Allan: What am I going to do with just the house? Seven.

Istvan: Six.

Allan: We haven't had it on the market for that long. Maybe
we should wait and see.

Istvan: Don't look a horse.

Allan: *Looking around.* What horse?

Istvan: A horse's teeth. Don't look a horse.

Allan: Oh! You mean, "Don't look a gift horse in the mouth."

Istvan: How many people knocked on door? Three? Two? One?
Allan does not answer. Five-fifty.

Allan: Five-fifty? You just said six.

Istvan: Five-twenty-five.

Allan: You can't go down!

Istvan: Five-fifteen, final offer.

Allan: You're supposed to meet me halfway!

Istvan: Five-ten. Final, final.

Allan: All right, all right. Six. I'll sever the house and sell it separate.

Istvan: Four-eighty.

Allan: Six!

Istvan and Allan shake hands on the deal. Charlotte wanders upstage to the raspberry patch. Allan regards his hand. He looks up at the audience.

Allan: A hundred years of farming this same spot, and for what? *Allan pulls a few loose bills out of his pocket.* Four generations, and it comes down to something you can hold in your hand. From a piece of land that your ancestors carved out of the wilderness and built a mud hut on, to … paper. It's like … what d'you call it? … like alchemy. I changed dirt into gold.

Well, fool's gold. These days money has no relationship whatsoever to the earth that it tries to describe, that it tries to put a value on. In a few years, with expenses, rise in the cost of living, bad investments — heck, just with inflation alone — the money that this farm was transformed into … will be gone. Now *that* … that's alchemy.

Charlotte emerges from the raspberry patch.

Charlotte: The day after Istvan bought the farm —

Allan: He bought the farm? But he was looking so healthy!

Charlotte: The day after Istvan bought the farm *from us*, we started looking at condos in the city.

*Lights: Allan becomes a **Real Estate Agent**.*

Real Estate Agent: This is our standard unit for this complex!

Living room, dining room, kitchen and on the left, TV room. Or playroom for the grandchildren. Any grandchildren?

Charlotte: No.

Real Estate Agent: Any on the way?

Charlotte: I don't think so.

Real Estate Agent: TV room, then. Two bedrooms through here. And a third guest room in the basement!

Allan: Basement? This isn't like a condo at all. More like a little house.

Charlotte: Allan was expecting a one-room roach motel.

Allan: Well that's what the boy had.

Charlotte: That's different.

Allan: That was a condo.

Charlotte: That was an apartment.

Allan: Then why did he pay condo fees?

Charlotte: Well ... it was ... an apartment-style condo. This is ... a condo-style condo.

Allan: *Muttering.* Not like a condo at all.

Charlotte: Shush, now. The nice lady's speaking.

Allan becomes the Real Estate Agent.

Real Estate Agent: There's a little sundeck off the back, with a lovely view of the park!

Charlotte: Oh, that is pretty. I can plant some nasturtiums right along the fence there.

Real Estate Agent: Ah. The landscaping is all provided for.

Charlotte: I don't mind. Not one little bit.

Real Estate Agent: The landscaping is all provided for. So that it looks nice.

Charlotte: Don't you worry. I'll put in something nice.

Real Estate Agent: I mean, so that it looks nice.

Charlotte: So you mean I can't …?

Real Estate Agent: You can plant whatever you want on the deck!

Charlotte: Just pots and window boxes then.

Real Estate Agent: Umm …

Charlotte: No window boxes?

Real Estate Agent: I'm afraid not. The landscaping is all provided for. It's all included in the condo fees.

Charlotte: Lord love a duck.

Charlotte becomes the Real Estate Agent.

Allan: What else is included in those condo fee things?

Real Estate Agent: Well, the basics. Utilities — gas and electricity — cable fees, high-speed internet —

Allan: I'm not gonna use the internet. Can you take that off?

Real Estate Agent: No. Landscaping, lawn maintenance, and snow removal. Also major repairs to the outside. They repainted last summer. This summer they're redoing all the downspouts!

Allan: Good to have new eavestroughs, I guess.

Real Estate Agent: Not the eaves. Just the downspouts. Your fees also include access to the clubhouse!

Allan: Clubhouse?

Real Estate Agent: In the centre of the whole complex there's a clubhouse, just like in Florida! There's a swimming pool, a gym, a billiard room, a bridge room —

Allan: Don't play bridge, can you take —?

Real Estate Agent: No. Once a week they play bingo instead of bridge.

Allan: At least I don't have to mow the grass.

Charlotte: Or shovel the walk. You shouldn't be shoveling the walk at your age.

Allan: Oh, Charlotte.

Charlotte: Ninety-five percent of people your age die of a heart attack while they're shoveling the walk.

Allan: Ninety-five percent? Is that right, Mother? If ninety-five percent of people my age die of a heart attack while they're shoveling the walk, do you mind telling me why there are *sooo* many people my age still walking around?

Charlotte: Of the people your age who die of a heart attack, ninety-five percent of them have that heart attack while they're shoveling the walk.

Allan: That's not what you said the first time.

Charlotte: That's what I meant.

Allan: But that's not what you said.

Charlotte: Listen to what I mean, not what I say.

Allan: You're always after *me* to say what I mean.

Charlotte: *To the audience.* He was like this the whole time we were buying the condo. It's a miracle we settled on anything at all. But settle we did. *To Allan.* If we're going to live in the city, we'll have to do something with that house.

Allan: Don't be so hasty there, Mother.

Charlotte: What are we going to do with a farmhouse that has no farm?

Allan: We don't need to get rid of everything all at once, do we?

Charlotte: A house that has no one living in it comes to no good. Just look at the old Bakker place, it's falling to pieces.

Allan: We can make some easy money from the rent.

Charlotte: What do you want to be a landlord for?

Allan: Charlotte, I was born on this farm.

Charlotte: You were born in a hospital.

Allan: This farm has been in my family for one hundred and thirty-eight years.

Charlotte: Your father *bought* it.

Allan: From his cousin.

Charlotte: But what kind of person will we end up with?

*Charlotte puts on aviator glasses and becomes **Ron**. He's a young, clean-cut man of about thirty, and though he has an urban sensibility, it's clear he's trying on country life like an ill-fitting coat. Still, he's the kind of man who puts you at ease and makes you want to trust him.*

Throughout this next section, both Allan and Charlotte play Ron, alternating rapidly. To make things clear, I have used "A-Ron" for when Allan plays the character and "C-Ron" for Charlotte.

A-Ron: Ron McKillop.

Charlotte: Charlotte Duncanson.

A-Ron: Mrs. Duncanson.

Charlotte: Please, call me Charlotte.

A-Ron: All right then. Charlotte.

Charlotte: *Aside.* He seemed like a nice enough fellow.

A-Ron: These might very well be the nicest flower beds in the whole county.

Charlotte: *Aside.* Uh-huh. A *real* nice fellow.

A-Ron: Don't tell the neighbours. They might get jealous.

Charlotte giggles, flattered.

C-Ron: I bet it's got good soil too. Not too much clay.
    Am I right?

Allan: *Aside.* Yep, he was a *real* nice fellow.

C-Ron: Nicest farm I've seen, anyway.

Allan: *Aside.* Had a good job.

C-Ron: I'm an airline pilot. Just got transferred out here.
    I've been checking out the countryside a bit.

Allan: Nice day.

C-Ron: Yep.

Allan: Yep.

C-Ron: Yep.

Allan: Yep, yep, yep.

C-Ron: Just look at the way that sun picks up the gold in
    those trees.

Allan: Winter's on its way.

C-Ron: Winter? Don't rush it. We're not even into fall yet.

Allan: We had frost last week.

C-Ron: Tell me about it.

Allan: See those aspen there? When that tree turns gold, then
    I know the first snow is just around the corner.

C-Ron: Is that right?

Allan: Yep. You here about the house?

C-Ron: I see from the paper that it's for rent.

Allan: Not a lot of people want to live out in the country any-more. Seems there's more space than people out here these days.

C-Ron: That's exactly what we are looking for.

Allan: I've worked this farm my whole life. Look out there. The row of trees hugging the crick, another line of trees here, making a natural windbreak for the house. The acre and a —

Ron abruptly interrupts Allan's poetic reverie.

C-Ron: You know, I missed all of that growing up in the city. You don't pay much attention to the seasons when you're in the city, except when it makes you late for work. Out here... Well, out here, the seasons, the weather, I guess it's a part of you.

A-Ron: How many rooms has it got?

Charlotte: Three bedrooms, kitchen, dining room, living room with fireplace. Downstairs there's two big rooms ...

A-Ron: That right?

Charlotte: Yep.

A-Ron: Both developed?

Charlotte: Well, the one's just a glorified storeroom, but it's got carpet and the walls are finished. That's where I keep one of them "rat races."

A-Ron: A which?

Charlotte: A rat race. One of those machines that you walk on all day, but never get anywhere. For exercise.

A-Ron: You mean a treadmill.

Charlotte: No, I mean a rat race. That's what I call it. "I'm gonna go join the rat race now."

A-Ron: I've had just about enough of the rat race. That's what I want to get away from.

Charlotte: The other room makes a nice TV room.

Allan: Mother made me renovate it a few years back. It used to have that maple veneer. And that nice orange shag carpet with the big black circles. Big as dinner plates.

C-Ron: *Laughs.* Nice. Right out of Austin Powers. "Yeah baby."

Allan is offended at the thought of someone mocking his beloved shag carpet.

Allan: It had some good years in it yet. I says to Charlotte, "Don't know why you have to go rip out perfectly good carpet when it's done all right by us for the past thirty years."

Charlotte: But I told him, "I'm not gonna watch TV down there with that d—— carpet."

A-Ron: I don't see any windows down there.

Charlotte: They're around on the back side. You can't see 'em from the road.

A-Ron: That'll work.

Charlotte: Pardon?

A-Ron: I'll take it.

Charlotte: Don't you want the grand tour? See the inside?

A-Ron: I brought the rent.

Ron hands Charlotte a thick wad of cash.

Charlotte: Oh, my. That's … cash. A cheque would have been fine, you know.

Ron: I don't have any cheques on me.

Charlotte: I don't mind saying that I'm kind of nervous having this much cash all at once.

Allan: Well, cash is still money after all.

Charlotte: There's just … a lot of it. You sure you couldn't give us a cheque?

A-Ron: I haven't been able to open a bank account out here yet. Some sort of problem with the computers.

Charlotte: What airline do you fly for?

A-Ron: WestJet. "Six flights to Toronto every day." [2]

Charlotte: Six flights? Imagine that.

Allan: Wouldn't think there'd be that many people that would want to go to Toronto.

C-Ron: Maybe they go to take in a game.

A-Ron: See the Blue Jays win one.

Charlotte: I suppose. Or family.

A-Ron: Sam — that's my wife — she works for the airline too; she's a stewardess.

Charlotte: I thought they called them flight attendants these days?

A-Ron: Huh?

Charlotte: A woman on Air Canada told Allan calling her a "stewardess" was sexist. Gave Allan a real talking-to.

A-Ron: That's Air Canada for you. So uptight they'd split a seam if they bent over to pick up a quarter.

Charlotte: We're a bit of a ways from the city.

A-Ron: Sure are.

Charlotte: About an hour from the airport. It's quite the commute.

Allan: Especially in winter.

C-Ron: … I work lots of overnight trips.

A-Ron: Gone for days at a time,

C-Ron: then three days off.

A-Ron: When I'm off,

C-Ron: I like to be *off.*

A-Ron: If you know what I mean.

Charlotte: You have to stay overnight on a flight to Toronto?

A-Ron: ... I don't do Toronto. I do the Las Vegas run.

Charlotte: And you have to stay over?

A-Ron: You can only fly so many hours at a time. Like truckers. Only more regulated.

Charlotte: It's just that ... Las Vegas doesn't seem that far. I don't see why the airline makes you stay over.

A-Ron: ... Doesn't make much sense to me either, Mrs. Duncanson.

Charlotte: Charlotte.

A-Ron: Charlotte.

Allan: *Counting the cash.* This is three months' rent.

Charlotte: We only need first and last month's rent.

A-Ron: I must have misunderstood.

Charlotte: Well, here you take that —

A-Ron: Why don't you just keep the three months? Then you won't need to come out as often.

Charlotte: We don't mind.

A-Ron: It's a long ways.

Charlotte: We're used to the drive.

A-Ron: I insist.

Charlotte: You young people have more important things you can spend that money on. You just tell Sam to buy something nice for herself.

A-Ron: ...OK, Mrs. Duncanson.

Charlotte: Charlotte.

A-Ron: Charlotte.

C-Ron: The utilities in your name?

Allan: It's all included in the rent.

C-Ron: We're not used to the cold. Probably be keeping it warm.

Allan: You go right ahead.

C-Ron: OK.

Pause.

A-Ron: Listen, I gotta split. Here's my cellphone number. Give me a call if there's anything else.

Ron hands Charlotte his card.

Charlotte: Oh, OK. When are you moving in?

A-Ron: Tomorrow?

Charlotte: Tomorrow?

A-Ron: I have a couple of flights back-to-back, and I want to make sure Sam has a place to stay.

Charlotte: Well, we've got most of our things at the condo already... How about the day after?

A-Ron: That'd be great. Sam tells me the truck will be arriving ... that day.

Charlotte: Well, let us know if you need a hand or anything.

A-Ron: *A little too quickly.* No! I mean — we'll be fine. Thanks. It was nice meeting you, Mrs. Duncans — Charlotte.

Charlotte: Give my best to Sam.

A-Ron: Yeah, I will. Bye.

Charlotte: Goodbye.

Allan: Bye.

Charlotte: *Aside.* And that ... was that.

Lights. We are in Allan and Charlotte's condo; they are unpacking boxes.

Allan: It seems odd to move away and never see it again.

Charlotte: We don't want to be nosy landlords. We have to let go. It isn't good for us to hang on.

Allan: Better to make a clean break.

Charlotte: Be done with it.

Pause. They unpack a few more boxes.

Allan: Course, we're not done with it.

Charlotte: Not really.

Allan: We've only rented it.

Charlotte: Still have to sell it.

Allan: Can't sell it if it isn't kept in good shape.

Charlotte: Well, we're not going. We're staying here.

Allan: At the new condo.

Charlotte: We have more than enough to keep us busy in the new place —

Allan: — without running off to the farm every few days.

Pause. They unpack a few more boxes.

Charlotte: I've never seen so many boxes. Seems like you unpack five or six and the next day a dozen more have sprouted up in the storeroom. Like rabbits.

Allan: You can almost hear them mating at night. Ever heard the sound of two boxes mating? All that cardboard rubbing together.

Charlotte: Allan!

Pause. They unpack a few more boxes.

Allan: You've gotta wonder how the water garden is doing.

Charlotte: You worked hard on that garden.

Allan: It'd be real easy for someone who doesn't know any better to forget to clean the algae out of the water pump.

Charlotte: Or to feed the fish.

Allan: Those koi sure do eat a lot.

Short pause. Charlotte chews her lower lip.

Charlotte: I bet the raspberries are out.

Allan spies the opening and jumps on it.

Allan: It would be a shame to let the birds get all those berries.

Charlotte: We could go and just pick the raspberries.

Allan: And check the water garden.

Charlotte: We don't have to bother them at all.

Allan: They don't even need to know we're there.

Allan and Charlotte look at each other. Lights. Charlotte is picking berries. Istvan appears (played by Allan).

Istvan: Something fishy.

Charlotte: Lord love a duck, Istvan! You scared the living daylights out of me!

Istvan: Horny Tim.

Charlotte: What?

Istvan: Too much Horny Tim. Bad coffee anyway. Drink tea.

Charlotte: I'll try that.

Istvan: *Indicates the house offstage.* Something fishy.

Charlotte: Did something happen to the koi?

Istvan: Koi?

Charlotte: The fish? In the water garden?

Istvan: No. Him fishy.

Charlotte: Who? Ron?

Istvan: Him and the other guy.

Charlotte: Other guy?

Istvan: All day inside. Even when weather nice.

Charlotte: There's nothing unusual in that.

Istvan: They Greek.

Charlotte: With a name like McKillop?

Istvan: No, *Greek.* Like "the boys" who run the quilting store.

Istvan raises his eyebrows and hangs his hand in a limp-wristed way.

Not welcoming those kinds here.

Charlotte: Now you just wait a minute. Those boys down at the
    quilting shop have never harmed a soul. They come to
    our church. They came once, anyway, for the strawberry
    social. And they were very polite. One of them grew up
    near here, down by Beisker, and his father was a United
    Church minister.

Istvan: United Church ... Feh!

Charlotte: They moved out here to get away from the city and
    to try to make a living for themselves in a nice honest
    way, and there is no point in making it any more difficult
    for them than it already is. And if this Ron and his ...

friend … if they're that way too, and if he was too … shy … or whatever … to tell us, well, then it's no wonder with attitudes like yours running rampant everywhere!

Istvan: *Defensively.* I'm not wanting to be breaking up the neighbourhoodliness. I just be saying —

Charlotte: They pay their rent and they're more than welcome, like anyone else. Now, if you'll excuse me.

Istvan: Just watch out for. That house — is still home.

Istvan leaves. Charlotte is both furious and concerned. After a moment:

Charlotte: Allan. Allan! Allan!!!

Charlotte dashes off down one side of the raspberry patch in search of her husband. Ron appears in the garden. He is wearing pink gardening gloves and holds a trowel.

A-Ron: Mrs. Duncanson.

Charlotte: Oh. Hello, Ron. You can call me Charlotte.

A-Ron: Right. Charlotte.

Charlotte is immediately nervous after her previous conversation: it's not like she's afraid he's going to bite her, but still, she is not sure how to speak to a gay person. She might even have trouble looking him in the eye.

Charlotte: What are you … what are you up to?

A-Ron: I am weeding the flower beds. I want to make sure you don't have to come around again.

Charlotte: Uh-huh. I like your gloves.

A-Ron: *Laughing.* Oh, yeah. I found them under the sink. Are they yours?

Charlotte: You can keep them.

A-Ron: Thanks.

Awkward pause.

Charlotte: Do you ... like flowers?

A-Ron: Uh, sure. Flowers are cool. To tell you the truth,
I'm starting to get a bit of a green thumb.

Awkward pause.

Charlotte: And cooking? Do you like to cook?

A-Ron: I make a mean stir-fry. But not much else.

Charlotte: And ... quilting?

A-Ron: Quilting?

Charlotte: Do you like to quilt?

A-Ron: Quilt?

Charlotte: *Frustrated.* It's a simple question, Ron, do you like
to quilt or don't you? Because if you do, there is a nice
quilting store in town run by two very nice boys, and
I thought you might like to drop in and look at them —
er — around, look around.

A-Ron: OK... Thanks for the advice.

Awkward pause. Finally, Charlotte decides to just be direct.

Charlotte: Ron, the person who's living with you isn't really
named Samantha ... is he?

A-Ron: Uh ... no. I'm sorry Mrs. D, I was going to tell you, but —

Charlotte: No. You don't have to explain to me. Or to anyone,
for that matter. What you do in the privacy of your own
home is your business and don't you dare let anyone in this
township tell you otherwise. Like Pierre Trudeau said, the
government has no place in the bedrooms of the people,
and I'll go one further and say the people have no place in
the bedrooms of the people. I've never been a Liberal, but
if there's one thing that man did right, it was keeping everyone out of everyone else's bedroom. So you just — you just —
you — you and your friend can just stay put and that's final.

A-Ron: OK. Thanks, Mrs. Duncanson.

Charlotte: Charlotte.

A-Ron: Right. Charlotte.

Charlotte turns to go, remembers something, and turns back.

Charlotte: What is your friend's name? Really? You can tell me.

A-Ron: Razor.

Charlotte: That's a nice — Razor?

A-Ron: Razor.

Charlotte: Well. Give my regards to Razor, then.

Charlotte leaves. Allan appears.

Allan: Razor?

Charlotte: That's what Ron said.

Allan: Did you meet this Razor?

Charlotte: No. And I won't need to either.

Allan: We have a "gay" named Razor living in our homestead and you don't feel curious enough to meet him?

Charlotte: Nope.

Allan: I wonder how many tattoos *Razor* has?

Charlotte: Let he who has not sinned cast the first stone.

Allan: It's not stones I'm worried about. It's orgies.

Charlotte: This Ron is a nice boy. He was weeding the garden. I'm sure it's fine. Besides, we don't —

Allan: — don't want to be nosy landlords, I know, I know. *Muttering:* Ron and Razor sitting in a tree, K-I-S-S-I-N-G ...

Charlotte: Allan!

Allan and Charlotte turn to the audience.

Allan: I suppose it was about a month later —

Charlotte: More than a month.

Allan: It was the end of the first month.

Charlotte: We found out about Razor on the first, which was a Tuesday. The next Sunday was the bake sale at the church, and the Sunday after that Reverend Carter went on vacation for two weeks, and that was when we had that nice woman preacher from up Seaforth way, the one who nearly gave Jean MacMullen a heart attack when she said God might have been a woman. So it was the Sunday after that.

Allan: So it *was* a month.

Charlotte: And five days.

Allan: So a month!

Charlotte: More like five weeks.

Allan: *Sighs.* Five weeks after Charlotte defended the honour of our suddenly gay tenant, Charlotte went to church. By herself. I had a Lions Club breakfast.

Charlotte: D—— Lions Club breakfast.

Allan: Which I have every fourth Sunday —

Charlotte: More important than church.

Allan: — which after thirty-odd years should not have come as a surprise to anyone!

Charlotte: Don't know why you can't find a Lions Club in the city.

Allan: Probably for the same reason you can't find a church in the city. And on this particular Sunday we had a vote on something or other. Sinclair — we always seem to be on opposite ends of any issue Clair and I — we had gotten into an argument over it. So I admit I left the meeting pretty distracted.

Charlotte: He was supposed to pick me up at church.

Allan: It was the strangest thing. You know how sometimes you can be driving along the highway in your truck thinking about the weather, and how summer seems to be so much shorter than it used to be when you were a child; how the summer days seemed to stretch out forever in those days, how there seemed to be enough time to do everything in a single day; time for the morning chores, time to play, time to build a treehouse and time to paint it too, time for supper, after-dinner chores, time to watch my father castrate the pigs, time for a bath and a story at bedtime … and how kids today want everything all at once, don't seem to want to work for it even, feel that if they don't get $40,000 starting salary fresh out of university then they're a failure — when all of a sudden … you realize that you've been driving on autopilot, not paying any attention to where you were going … and all of a sudden …

Pause, while Allan takes in the sight of the beloved farm.

Well, I'll be goldarned. Just drove straight to the old homestead. Like a horse that bucked its rider and just wanders home.

Well, might as well check the pump while I'm here.

Allan bends down to check the water garden, muttering to himself.

Look at this, the pump is clogged. Has been for some time. The motor's fine. Had the smarts to turn it off when it clogged. Oh, look at this … one of the koi is dead.

Allan looks at the dead fish. He is devastated.

Tsk, tsk, tsk. Poor little Hoi. Hoi Polloi, the koi. He was always so arrogant.

Only Neil left. He ain't doing too well either. There's a great blue heron out here that comes along every once in a while … tries to eat the fish. Frankly, I'm surprised they lasted as long as they did. Can't leave poor old Neil all alone. Not with that heron out to get him. Only one thing left to do.

Allan knocks on the door. A dog starts barking within the house and thumps against the door, angry, frothing. Charlotte puts on the aviator glasses and becomes Ron. She shouts through the closed door.

C-Ron: Who is it?

Allan: It's Allan.

C-Ron: Who?

Allan: Allan.

C-Ron: There's no Allan here.

Allan: No, I'm Allan.

C-Ron: You got the wrong house, buster.

Allan: It's *Allan.* Your landlord.

C-Ron: Landlor —? Oh! Hey.

The dog is still barking loudly. Ron tries to quiet it. Quiet. Shh. Heel.

Allan: I didn't know you had a dog.

Allan & C-Ron: Sorry.

C-Ron: I guess I should have told you.

Allan: No, sorry, I didn't mean to be a nosy landlord. My fault. None of my business. Have a dog if you want.

The dog is still barking loudly.

C-Ron: Quiet. Heel.

Allan: I wonder if I could borrow a shovel?

C-Ron: A shovel?

Allan: One of the koi died.

C-Ron: The what?

Allan: The fish. One of the fish died.

C-Ron: Oh, yeah, I noticed that.

Allan: You did, eh?

C-Ron: Yeah.

Allan: Well, I'm not sure it was a good idea to let him float there. *Pause.* So I thought I'd bury him. *Pause.* I wonder if I could borrow a shovel.

C-Ron: I ain't got no shovel.

Allan: Are you all right, Ron?

C-Ron: Yeah, just … a late night. *The dog is still barking loudly.* Shut up. Stupid dog.

Allan: Flight got in late?

C-Ron: What? Oh, yeah, late flight. Don't you have a shovel in that barn over there?

Allan: No. I sold the barn. It went with the farm. I don't suppose you have a bucket?

C-Ron: A bucket?

Allan: I should take the other fish somewhere else. Where he can be looked after.

C-Ron: Sure, I got a bunch of buckets.

Ron goes back inside. Allan instinctively tries to step inside the house, but the dog starts to growl. Allan tries to resist glancing in inside, but after a moment he sneaks a peek. The dog growls more. Allan starts to back up. The dog starts to bark. Allan is concerned. Ron returns with a bucket. He has to restrain the dog.

C-Ron: Here you go. *To the dog.* Stop it. Stop!

Allan: Thanks. You don't … uh … you don't seem to have much in the way of furniture in there.

C-Ron: ... The furniture's been delayed.

Allan: Delayed? I thought the truck was arriving the day you moved in?

C-Ron: The truck ... had an accident. The moving company tried to get another one, but ... it's been taking a while.

Allan: I'll say. It's been weeks. That's outrageous.

C-Ron: ... We didn't want to pay the premium price, so we went for the cheaper option, which is a bit slower.

Allan: The airline wasn't paying?

C-Ron: ... only up to a certain amount.

Allan: Right. So ...

C-Ron: So, we wanted it to be cheaper.

Allan: Still ... no furniture.

C-Ron: We don't mind. It's kind of like camping.

Allan: Right.

The dog is still barking. Ron loses his temper — he swats at the dog violently.

C-Ron: Shut the hell up. Shut up! Shut up! Shut up! *Ron notices Allan staring at him.* I'm just looking after it for a friend.

Allan: Razor?

C-Ron: Yeah. Razor. I'm not a dog person, I ... it's driving me nuts. Damn thing.

Allan: Well. Let us know if you need anything.

C-Ron: Sure. Sorry about the fish.

Allan: Yeah. He was a ... a good little fella. He'll be missed.

Lights; back at the condo.

Well, that was strange.

Charlotte: What did you do with the dead fish?

Allan: I left him for the blue heron.

Charlotte: Allan! You didn't leave a rotting fish on the lawn?

Allan: ... No. I put him behind a bush.

Charlotte: Lord love a duck.... You didn't bring the other fish home, did you?

Allan: ... No.

Charlotte: Good.

Allan surreptitiously nudges the bucket to one side.

Not a stick of furniture?

Allan: I didn't see the whole house.

Charlotte: You didn't go in?

Allan: He had a dog.

Charlotte: A dog?

Allan: Didn't want to be a nosy landlord.

She nods in agreement.

Charlotte: When Elizabeth was at college, she went a whole year without a teapot. Don't know how she managed.

Allan: That's a teapot. These folks don't have *furniture*.

Charlotte: Do you think we should take them some?

Allan: We have that pull-out couch downstairs. And that rocking chair of mother's that you hate so much.

Charlotte: We could go to the thrift store and get a coffee table. Maybe a TV.

Allan: Good Lord! You think they don't have a TV?

Charlotte: I sure hope so. I could take them a casserole.

Allan: Maybe the Lion's Club has a few things that didn't sell at the rummage sale.

Charlotte: Still … we don't want to be nosy landlords.

Allan nods in agreement.

Allan: They can take care of themselves.

Charlotte nods in agreement.

We wouldn't want to be nosy landlords.

Pause.

Charlotte: How were the flower beds?

Allan: I didn't notice.

Charlotte: What do you mean you didn't notice?

Allan: I didn't see.

Charlotte: How can you not see? They're right there in front of the house.

Allan: I didn't look.

Charlotte shakes her head.

Charlotte: Allan Duncanson, I swear, sometimes you can't see the nose on your face. The electricity bill came today.

Charlotte hands Allan an unopened envelope.

Allan: Oh, finally.

Charlotte: I guess it takes a while for the change of address to take effect.

Allan: I guess. It's been a while, though.

Charlotte: Two months.

Allan: Has it been two months already, Mother?

Charlotte: I guess so, Father.

Allan: Are you enjoying your new house, Mother?

Charlotte: Aren't you?

Allan: ... Yes ... sure.

Charlotte: ... Me too.

Allan opens the envelope. He does a double take.

Allan: Holy cow!

Charlotte: What's that?

Allan: It's a bit high, is all. Holy cow!

Charlotte: Let me see — Lord love a duck!

Allan: *A bit too eagerly.* Do you think we'd better go have a talk with them?

They look at each other for an instant. Then they run and grab their coats. Lights. Allan and Charlotte approach the door. Allan is about to knock on the door when Charlotte interrupts.

Charlotte: Just let them know that we don't mean to be nosy, but electricity prices are increasing all the time.

Allan: Yes dear.

Allan is about to knock on the door when Charlotte interrupts again.

Charlotte: And that it's not their fault. We must not have been clear before.

Allan: It's our fault. Got it.

Allan is about to knock on the door when again Charlotte interrupts.

Charlotte: There's a fireplace. Tell them they could feel free to use the fireplace.

Allan: Are you done? Can I knock on the door now?

Charlotte: Shush. Just hurry up.

Allan knocks on the door. It creaks open. They both step back in shock, staring at the door. Ominous music builds.

Wasn't it locked?

Allan: The door just swung open when I knocked. The door jamb is broken, splintered right along the inside here.

Charlotte: Looks like someone has kicked the door in.

Allan: Charlotte, why don't you go wait in the car?

Charlotte: Maybe we should both go wait in the car.

Allan: You go. I'll catch up.

Charlotte: What are you going to do?

Allan: I'm going to take a little peek around.

Charlotte: I don't want you going in there all alone.

Allan: Charlotte, don't argue with me. Whoever did this might still be around.

Charlotte: That's why you shouldn't go in there alone.

Allan: Go on back to the car.

Charlotte: I haven't put up with you for forty-two years to have you get clubbed to death now.

Allan: Goldarnit, Charlotte Duncanson, in forty-two years you've never done a single thing I've told you to.

Charlotte: And I'm not about to start now. Wouldn't want you drop dead of a heart attack. Not when you're so hell-bent on getting clubbed to death.

Allan: Just … stay behind me.

Allan picks up a stick and brandishes it in front of him. It is small and pathetic, but it makes him feel better. They enter the house. The lights are dim and spooky.

Charlotte: Try the light switch.

Allan: Nothing. Must be burned out.

Charlotte takes a step. Something crunches under her feet. Glass. Allan looks up.

Look. The light wasn't burned out. It's been smashed.

Charlotte: Do you think they were robbed?

Allan: Don't know. Hello? Hello?

Charlotte: Anybody home? Ron?

Allan: Let's call the police.

Charlotte: It might be nothing.

Allan: Nothing?

Charlotte: They might have *accidentally* kicked the door in. Maybe they forgot their key.

Allan: Let's call the police.

Charlotte takes another few steps.

Charlotte: Why's it so cold?

Allan: Still no furniture, see.

The door slams shut behind them.

Charlotte: Ah! What was that?

Allan: I don't know.

Charlotte: The door! The door's been slammed shut. There's someone in here.

Allan: Shh.

Silence. They listen. The ominous music kicks up a notch.

Charlotte: Allan?

Allan: Yes?

Charlotte: I love you, Allan. I just realized … I don't know the last time I told you that.

Silence. They listen.

Allan?

Allan: What?

Charlotte: Aren't you going to say something?

Pause, while Allan thinks.

Allan: Oh! I love you too.

Charlotte: About time.

Allan: Sorry, I was a bit distracted.

Silence. They listen.

Charlotte: Do you hear anyone?

Allan: No. I think it was just the wind.

Charlotte: The wind? From where?

Allan: The window's open. The curtains are drawn, but the window's open. See?

Charlotte: Maybe that's why the electricity bill's so high?

Relieved, Allan starts off again. After one step he freezes.

Allan: Oh geez.

Charlotte: What is it?

Allan: I stepped in doo-doo.

Charlotte: What?

Allan: I stepped in dog doo-doo.

Charlotte: On the rug?

Allan: I wonder where that dog is?

Charlotte: I hope he wasn't hurt.

Allan: Hurt?

Charlotte: By the thieves. Do you think they would have hurt a dog?

Allan: After it did its business on the floor, I hope someone hurt it.

Charlotte: Shh. Do you hear that?

Allan: Which?

Charlotte: The furnace is on.

Allan: There's no heat coming out of the vent here.

Charlotte: I can hear the furnace.

Allan: I think it's just the fan. The heat's off, but the fan's on.

Charlotte: The fan? With the windows open?

Allan: Maybe. I don't know.

Charlotte: What's that smell?

Allan: Doo-doo. On my shoe.

Charlotte: No, no something else. Smells … musty.

Allan: I know that smell. I just can't place it …

Charlotte: Oh my God. What's that?

Allan: What?

Charlotte: On the walls. The walls are covered.

Allan: Go back to the car.

Charlotte: Is that blood?

Allan: I want you to go back to the car.

Charlotte: They've been murdered and their blood's been smeared all over the walls!

Allan: Go back to the car.

Charlotte: *Taking a deep breath.* Just shush up and find a light.

Allan flicks on a light switch. Pause. They stare at the wall blankly.

What is that?

Allan starts to move closer. He reaches out to touch the wall.

Allan: It's … I think it's …

Charlotte: What? It's what?

Allan: I think it's mould.

Charlotte: Mould?

Allan: Mould.

Charlotte: No.

Allan: It's mould, all right.

Charlotte: How can all the windows be open and yet the walls are covered in mould?

Lights. Charlotte picks up the phone. Ron answers in a tight spot. He is extremely nervous. He keeps his voice low and he keeps checking over his shoulder, as if he is hiding from someone. He might be in a closet or on a window ledge; either way, he's in trouble.

Ron: Ron here.

Charlotte: Hello? Ron?

Ron: Yeah. Talk fast.

Charlotte: *Speaking quickly* Ronit'sCharlotteDuncanson.

Ron's demeanour suddenly changes. He's like a kid who's been caught by the teacher.

Ron: Hi, Mrs. Duncanson!

Charlotte: Call me Charlotte.

Ron: Hello, Charlotte.

Charlotte: We're standing at the house.

Ron: You are.

Charlotte: And there's something wrong with the door.

Ron: I was going to call you about that. Someone broke in while we were away. ... We aren't real comfortable staying there anymore.

Charlotte: You aren't?

Ron: We'll pay until the end of the month. Next month if you want. But we don't feel safe ... With people breaking in and all.

Charlotte: So ...

Ron: So we've moved out.

Charlotte: You've moved out? Already?

Ron: Yes ma'am. Sorry we didn't give you more notice. I shampooed the rug.

Charlotte: You shampooed the rug?

Ron: I thought it was the least I could do.

Charlotte: There's dog doo-doo on the rug.

Ron: There is? That must have been ... my friend's dog.

Charlotte: Razor?

Ron: Yeah, Razor. I didn't know nothing about that. I shampooed the rug. I was trying to do the right thing.

Charlotte: What "right thing"?

Ron: The — Nothing. I'm sorry is all, Mrs. Duncanson.

Charlotte: Call me Charlotte.

Ron: I'm sorry, Charlotte. I really am.

Charlotte: Ron, why is there mould on the walls? *Silence.* Ron?

Silence. Ron?

Ron is gone. Charlotte hangs up the phone. She turns to Allan. Pause. Lights.

I was pregnant with our first when we finished building that house. And I was pregnant with our second when we put that G-blankety-blank carpet down in the basement. We raised two children in that house. And now ...

Charlotte starts to cry. Allan tries to comfort her.

Allan: There, there ...

Charlotte: Oh, Allan, what's going to happen to our home?

Allan: We'll find out soon enough.

Allan and Charlotte pick up a few boxes and head offstage away from the house, towards the car. Lights.

INTERMISSION

ACT TWO

Allan begins Act Two just as he began Act One: pacing and waiting for bad news. He keeps glancing offstage left, into the distance. Allan stops, sighs, and looks down at the ground. He looks up and squints out at the audience. Before he can speak, Charlotte enters with a box.

Allan: Any sign of him?

Charlotte: Nothing.

Allan: Nothing?

Charlotte: Nothing.

Allan: Surely there must be something by now.

Charlotte: Well, if you don't like what I say, then quit asking me. All I know is he hasn't come out of the house, and that's all I have to tell you.

Allan: OK. OK. OK.

Allan wanders off left. Charlotte shouts after him.

Charlotte: You're not going in there and that's final.

Allan: OK. OK. OK.

Charlotte: Just finish the story.

Allan: *Pouting.* I don't remember where I was.

Charlotte: We had no sooner finished calling Ron than we
called the police. An officer came right away. Not that he
and Allan got much done.

*Lights. Charlotte becomes the **Policeman**.*

Allan: So …

Policeman: So …

Allan: So …

Policeman: Are you related to the Duncansons up Largie way?

Allan: My grandmother came from that way.

Policeman: Then you might know my Aunt Patty.

Allan: Oh, Patty, yeah, sure. You a MacMillian, then?

Policeman: No, I'm a Patton.

Allan: Then your father must be Dwight.

Policeman: Daryl. Dwight's my uncle.

Allan: That's right. Dwight married Patty and Daryl married —

Policeman: Patty's twin sister Pam.

Allan: Patty's the homely one.

Policeman: Well, they *are* twins.

Allan: So, how's Pam doing?

Policeman: She had a heart attack two years ago.

Allan: Sorry to hear that.

Policeman: Yep.

Allan: Yep.

Policeman: Yep.

Allan: Yep, yep, yep.

Charlotte drops the persona of the Policeman.

Charlotte: *Frustrated.* OK, that's it, let me talk to him.

Allan: What do you mean?

Charlotte: Lord love a duck, we'll be here all day at this rate.

Allan takes the hat and adopts the persona of the Policeman.

Policeman: So, you got some mould?

Charlotte: All over the walls. Upstairs and down.

The Policeman nods knowingly.

Policeman: Grow-op.

Charlotte: Excuse me?

Policeman: Dope.

Charlotte smiles blankly; she has no idea what he is talking about.

Mary Jane. Ganja. Smoke. Grass. Weed. Pot. Marijuana.

Charlotte: Oh! Marijuana. What about it?

Policeman: Someone used your house to grow marijuana.

Charlotte: Not our house.

Policeman: I'm afraid so.

Charlotte: Well, who would do that?

Policeman: You said you had been renting the house out?

Charlotte: Yes, but — no! You don't think —? Not Ron?

Policeman: More than likely.

Charlotte: They grow marijuana in Canada? I thought it was all over in Afghanistan or something.

Policeman: British Columbia is the biggest exporter of marijuana in the world.

Charlotte: British Columbia? But it's so pretty.

Policeman: You ever heard of Nelson, BC? According to Revenue Canada, fifty percent of the population lives below the poverty line. Take a drive around there sometime, check out all the big houses. There's a huge underground economy in that province of an unimaginable scale. No wonder they called it British *Columbia*. And you thought farming couldn't turn a profit!

Charlotte: I ... I feel faint. I have to sit down.

Policeman: Don't feel bad. Happens all the time.

The Policeman helps Charlotte sit down. In so doing, Charlotte deftly plucks the Policeman's hat from Allan and resumes the role of the Policeman.

We find three, maybe five operations a year. More, out near Brooks. Not surprising, really, when you think about what's going on in these communities. Farmers going bankrupt, folk retiring, people moving away left, right, and centre. All these empty houses. These days there's more space than people around these parts, and that's exactly what these operations are looking for.

Allan: So ... where'd the mould come from?

Policeman: Gotta keep it humid. Marijuana is a tropical plant.

Allan: Likes lots of rain, lots of moisture?

Policeman: They rig up huge UV lights over the whole shebang. Keep the lights on fourteen, fifteen hours a day. Until they're ready to harvest. Then they don't keep them on as much.

Allan: Fool the plants into thinking it's fall, force them to bud?

Policeman: Must have been amateurs.

Allan: Amateurs?

Policeman: Pros bypass the electrical meter.

Allan: Jack right into the power line.

Policeman: Heck, I heard of some teenagers the other day down in Claresholm who were growing it in Grandpa's barn.

Allan: Mormons?[3]

Policeman: Excommunicated Mormons now.

Allan: Guess so.

Policeman: Yep.

Allan: Yep.

Policeman: Yep. Yep. Yep. Even they were smart enough to bypass the meter.

Allan: Isn't that dangerous?

Policeman: Oooooooh yeah! It's usually badly wired. One short and the whole thing goes up in flames. That's how we catch ninety percent of them — they just set themselves on fire.

Allan: I guess we got lucky.

Charlotte leaps to her feet. This change is more instantaneous than the others, because she is so mad.

Charlotte: Lucky? You call this lucky? Look — just look — at this house. There's doo-doo on my carpet.

Policeman: Guard dog. Scare away unwanted visitors.

Charlotte: And the door. My front door.

Policeman: Yeah, that's a puzzler.

Charlotte: And the windows were wide open.

Policeman: Air the place out. That's why they left the fan going too. Cut down on the mould damage. Real nice of them.

Charlotte: Nice?!

Policeman: Worse if the windows were closed. Might not have done much, but at least they tried.

Charlotte: I'll be sure to thank them.

Charlotte walks away, disgusted. As she does so, she becomes the Policeman.

Allan: Well, there ain't no point in crying over spilt milk. I guess we might as well just clean up the mess.

Allan reaches out to touch the wall. The Policeman stops him.

Policeman: I wouldn't do that if I were you. Biggest problem with these grow houses is the mould.

Allan: Looks a bit thick, that's for sure.

Policeman: More than that. It's likely black mould.

Allan: Black mould? Isn't that …?

Policeman: Toxic.

Allan: Toxic?

Policeman: I'd be putting on some rubber gloves and a respirator before I touched that. I wouldn't touch it all. I'd get a hazardous materials team.

Allan: Hazardous materials?!

Policeman: Cost you about fifty, maybe seventy thousand.

Allan: Seventy thousand? Dollars!

Policeman: Maybe less. Maybe more. Frankly, I'd be talking to the insurance company before I did anything else.

Lights: the raspberry patch.

Charlotte: *Aside.* You never really think about insurance.

Allan: *Aside.* Until you need it.

Charlotte: *Aside.* Cudmore Farm Insurance.

Allan: *Aside.* I went to Ag School with Nesbitt Cudmore. Glasses thick as the bottoms of Coke bottles. Napoleon, we called him. Not on account of his size ... because of his greasy hair.

*Lights: the offices of the Local Farm Insurance Company. Allan shouts, almost sings, Nesbitt's nickname; **Nesbitt** winces.*

Allan: Naaaa-polllll-eon!!!

Nesbitt: You can call me Nesbitt, Allan. We're not in school anymore.

Allan: We seem to have had a spot of trouble, Napoleon.

Nesbitt: I've heard. A grow operation.

Allan: Hard to believe, isn't it?

Nesbitt: Not hard at all. This is the third such operation I've had to deal with in this county alone.

Allan: You're kidding.

Nesbitt: And all of those incidents were in houses owned by absentee landlords.

Allan: You'd think they'd know better.

Nesbitt: If you're going to rent, you can't be an absentee land-lord. It's irresponsible.

Allan: Irresponsible. That's a good word for it.

Nesbitt: So why did you do it?

Allan: Do which? Absentee landlord? Us? No, no, see, Nesbitt, the wife and me —

Nesbitt: Moved to the city.

Allan: Back in the summer. We got a real nice condo — Oh. Well, that's not being an absentee landlord ... Is it?

Nesbitt: How many times did you check on the house?

Allan: Oh well ... we didn't ... want to be nosy.

Nesbitt: Did you check your tenant's references?

Allan: ... Sure.

Nesbitt: You didn't, did you?

Allan: Didn't need to. He was an airline pilot.

Nesbitt: An airline pilot? Living out here?

Allan: He liked the farm. He wanted to commute.

Nesbitt: No one wants to commute from here, Allan.

Allan: No. I guess not.

Nesbitt opens a file folder on his desk.

Nesbitt: Were you aware, Allan, that you have a standard farm insurance protection plan?

Allan: Well, yes, of course.

Nesbitt: Not landlord-tenant insurance.

Allan: Oh.

Nesbitt: According to the Standard Farm Insurance Protection Plan, you are provided protection for — and here I quote, "liability insurance; machinery replacement; fire, theft or vandalism to outbuildings; hail damage; crop failure; and acts of God." Acts of God, not acts of tenants.

Allan: Now just a minute here.

Nesbitt: Technically, according to the terms of this insurance policy, you are not even allowed to *be* a landlord. In short, you are in breach of contract.

Allan: Meaning ...?

Nesbitt: Meaning that you have no insurance.

Allan: No insur —? Now just a minute.

Nesbitt pulls a letter out of his file.

Nesbitt: This letter here serves notice that henceforth our insurance is null and void.

Allan: Nesbitt, my family has been coming here for three generations. My father helped start this company in 1936.

Nesbitt: Technically, he helped start "The Local Farm Insurance *Co-operative*" —

Allan: *My father helped start this company.* We have been paying into this company even when it was a sacrifice to do so. We have never once made a claim on this insurance, not once in sixty-nine years.

Nesbitt: Technically, you can't claim your father's credit rating —

Allan: *If you say technically one more time I'll wring your neck!* Cleaning up that house is going to cost tens of thousands of dollars. Charlotte and I, we sold that farm for as much as we could get, and it's not much. This could wipe us out.

Nesbitt: I'm sure that —

Allan: I won't be able to retire. I'll be one of those sorry old saps, working at Wal-Mart until I'm ninety, helping strapping young women carry their microwaves to their SUVs.

Nesbitt: I'm sorry, Allan. I really am.

Allan: Nesbitt ... I'm begging you.

Pause. Nesbitt looks stricken. Nesbitt leaves. Allan is alone.

A hundred years of farming, and for what? We changed dirt into gold and now we've changed gold ... into mould. Alchemy.

Charlotte enters. She chuckles. Allan frowns. Charlotte nudges him. Reluctantly Allan smiles. They share a chuckle.

Charlotte: Even if we end up poor doesn't mean we can't still have a laugh. Probably it means we can have a better laugh.

Allan puts his arms around Charlotte. Lights. Organ music starts to play softly in the background. Charlotte looks forlorn, clutching her purse.

During the following sequence Allan will play four different women. There are many imaginative ways to stage this: hats, voices, puppets and even cardboard cut-outs are all welcome techniques.

Charlotte: *Forlornly.* Hello, Jean.

Jean: Charlotte, what's happened to your eyes?

Charlotte: Oh, nothing.

Jean: You've been crying. What's happened?

Charlotte: Never you mind.

Jean: Mary-Margaret, get yourself over here.

Charlotte: Don't trouble yourself, Mary-Margaret.

Mary-Margaret: Sadie, Geraldine. Come here for a second. Something's happened to Charlotte.

Sadie: Charlotte Duncanson, you tell us what's wrong.

Charlotte: If you insist, Sadie. You've heard about our troubles with the house?

Sadie: Oh, yes. Awful, that.

Charlotte: Well, that Nesbitt Cudmore has cancelled our insurance.

Sadie: No!

Charlotte: Yes.

Geraldine: No!

Charlotte: Yes, Geraldine. For him to treat us like that...

Geraldine: This kind of thing could have happened to
anybody.

Mary-Margaret: Jim McNeil, Sinclair Oldham, Ken Sheppard.

Sadie: We're all getting on in years.

Jean: Sooner or later we're all going to be too old to stay on
the land and those of us who can't sell their farms —

Sadie: — or won't —

Jean: — we're going to have to rent.

Charlotte: And those marijuana growers, they're sly.

Sadie: Sooner or later they'll get somebody else —

Mary-Margaret: — and then those folks'll be stuck with a bill
in the hundreds of thousands —

Sadie: — and no insurance to help them out when they need it.

Jean: This will never do. I'll tell my Sam that we're canceling
our insurance first thing Monday morning. And I'll have
Sam tell Sinclair too.

Mary-Margaret: Oh, Sinclair, he's all wind and blow.

Charlotte: I'll have a word with his wife Sharon. Once you've
told Sharon, then you might as well have told the whole
town.

Jean: And Ken Sheppard, get Sharon to call him too.

Sadie: Ken's a little slow, you'll have to work on him.

Geraldine: Take him one of your blueberry pies.

Charlotte: Clarence Dow.

Jean: Clarence Dow.

Sadie: Clarence Dow.

Mary-Margaret: Clarence Dow.

Geraldine: He runs the John Deere dealership.

Charlotte: If John Deere cancels its insurance, then that Nesbitt will really begin to worry.

Geraldine: Farmers who buy John Deere shop in packs.

Sadie: You never see a John Deere tractor with a Massey Ferguson plow, no sir.

Jean: They have conventions, those people.

Lights: the raspberry patch.

Charlotte: They say you can't take it with you — which is fine by me. If I never unpack another box in all my days, it'll be too soon — but if I could be standing at the pearly gates with those four women at my side, then I'd know that everything would be all right.

Allan comes up beside her and gives her shoulder a squeeze.

Charlotte: Oh, I'd want you by my side too, Allan.

Allan: Not if Jean MacMullen's going to be there. I'll make reservations at the other place.

Charlotte: Allan!

Lights. Allan stares out at the farm. Istvan sees him and wanders over to say a few words.

Istvan: I hear bad news about home.

Allan: We seem to have had a spot of trouble, Istvan.

Istvan: Bad news Greek boys.

Allan: They weren't Greek, Istvan. They were dope fiends.

Istvan: No!

Allan: Sure as I'm standing here in front of you.

Istvan: How is house? Bad? Very bad? *Allan doesn't answer.*
I am feeling the sorry.

Allan: Fifty thousand dollars to clean it up. Maybe more.

Istvan: Just tear down.

Allan: Then we pretty much have nothing.

Istvan: But you sell farm.

Allan: And spent the money on a condo in the city. I was
counting on the sale of the house to see us through.

Istvan: You have the pension.

Allan: CPP? For a farmer? Shoot me now.

Istvan: I was telling you already: never retire. Never you listen.
This your problem. Is like the llama. To me you say this
great idea. Untapped market for llama meat. To you I say,
market not tapped for good reason. But do you listen?
No, you have the idea, and the blinders, up they go. Like
horse. Not left, not right. Only see what you want. Plod
ahead, and over cliff. Like lemming.

Allan: I guess I've always had that problem.

Istvan: I say too much. But these things, you must be hearing
them.

*Silence between the two men. Allan stands. Istvan stands. They face
each other but do not shake hands: the truth is hard to face. Istvan
moves off.*

Lights: Allan stands in front of the grave of his mother.

Allan: Four generations of farming the same plot of land,
of turning the dirt into gold and investing the gold back
into the dirt again. From dust to dust, eh, Ma?

I used to come and visit Pa whenever I got into trouble
with the llamas, or whatever it was that time. Now I guess
it's your turn.

Remember that time the bank came to foreclose on the combine and the thresher? I knew they'd be coming, so I moved them down the road to cousin Don's place the night before. Hid them behind his barn. Didn't even tell him. Boy, you really blew a gasket when you found out, didn't you? "Don works for the Ministry of Agriculture. He'll never turn you in, he'll never even say a word of reproach to you. But look what you done to him. If his supervisor finds out, then he'll lose his job faster than you can say Jack Robinson." You remember saying that, Ma?

Guess I've always been too stubborn for my own good, ain't I?

Pause.

I don't think I ever told you that I handed the combine over, did I? I was too proud to tell you that I figured you were right. I figured that's what Pa would have done: handed everything over and taken his lumps.

You and Pa always managed somehow. Guess Charlotte and I will too. Maybe that job at Wal-Mart won't be so bad after all.

Allan stands up, ready to leave. Enter Nesbitt.

Shocked. Nesbitt. *Flinty.* Fancy meeting you here.

Nesbitt: I was just on my way to visit my father. *Pause.* He's over there with the rest of the Cudmores.

Allan: Don't let me stop you.

Nesbitt: When your mother died, I don't know if I ever told you how sorry I was for your loss, Allan.

Allan: Fine.

Nesbitt: Your mother was a client for seventy-one years. My father always said that if your parents hadn't invested their savings and talked it up to the neighbours, the

Local Farm Insurance Cooperative never would have gotten off the ground.

Remember when every business was local? The Co-op, the hardware store, the credit union. People like you and me would sit down over a cup of coffee and try to see what we could work out.

Allan, Cudmore hasn't been a local co-op insurer since the sixties. These days all insurance is run out of three or four big companies in Ontario.[4] They make all the decisions. I'm just the broker. I can't even change the colour of my sign. If your friends keep this up, they'll ruin me. Because you have a lot of friends. I'll lose what little I have. Please, Allan, I'm begging you.

Allan: I'll call off the dogs.

Nesbitt: Thank you. *They shake hands. Nesbitt leans in conspiratorially, as if someone might overhear them in the empty graveyard.* Get an assessment done.

Allan: Assessment?

Nesbitt: An Environmental Inspector's assessment. Maybe it's not really black mould.

Allan: And if it's not ... they'll cover the damage?

Nesbitt: No. But if it's not black mould ... maybe it won't cost as much. Maybe you'll still have your retirement.

Nesbitt shuffles off. Lights. Charlotte enters the coffee shop just as Ron is turning away from the counter with a coffee in hand and bumps into Charlotte.

Charlotte: I'll have a double double —

A-Ron: Just keep the change. Ooops.

Charlotte: Oh! Excuse me — Ron?

A-Ron: Charlotte?

Charlotte: You can call me Mrs. Duncanson.

A-Ron: I — I — I gotta go.

Ron starts to go. Charlotte stops him in his tracks.

Charlotte: Hold it right there, young man. I believe you owe me an explanation.

A-Ron: Mrs. Duncanson. I'm sorry. I really am. I didn't mean for anyone to get hurt.

Ron starts to go.

Charlotte: Ron. I have a cellphone in my hand. I have my finger on the nine. And pressing a pair of ones doesn't take very many seconds.

A-Ron: Charlotte — Mrs. Duncanson — they'll kill me if I say anything.

Charlotte: Who's that, dear?

A-Ron: You know. *Them.*

Charlotte: Why don't you sit down and tell me all about *them.*

A-Ron: I can't.

Charlotte: Well, then I guess I'd better let my fingers do the talking.

A-Ron: OK. OK. *They sit down at a table, over their coffees.* I have a confession to make: I am not really an airline pilot.

Charlotte: I think I figured that much out.

A-Ron: But I'm not a criminal either.

Charlotte: You ran a grow-op.

A-Ron: It was for my wife, Samantha … She has the chronic fatigue syndrome … nearly bedridden … and you know the only thing relieves the symptoms is —

Charlotte: Ron. I have just dialed two ones. Either you give me the truth or I press send.

A-Ron: The truth isn't very pretty, Char — Mrs. Duncanson.
The truth is that I've spent most of my life on the wrong
side of the law. I got a bit of problem with the bottle. And
with the pot. But none of the hard stuff. You spend as
much time as I do in bars and strip clubs, opportunities
start to come your way. Like when I met Razor. He told
me, "All you have to do is pick up a hockey bag from an
address in Red Deer that I'll give you, and hop the bus
to Ft. McMurray.[5] When you get off the bus, you go to
this other address. An easy five thousand dollars." And
he paid for the bus ticket.

So you do another ride. And another. And each one is
going to be the last, and then you'll quit. But on one of
those bus trips, I dipped into the package. And then I
started keeping some for myself. And then I figured, now
that I got all of Razor's contacts, why do I need Razor?

So I started growing my own. I got a book from the
library. I got pretty good at it too … until Razor found
out I had cut him out of the deal. That's when I found
out that Razor is a big tough guy who is in a club — with
a bunch of other big tough guys. They set me up with a
plot in the woods. But then the first frost hit in *September*.
Ruined half the crop. Razor told me he was going to
take it out of my hide. I thought he was just joking at
first, but … *Ron rolls up his sleeve and reveals a long scar.*

Razor doesn't joke around. That's when I found you.

Charlotte: I thought Razor was your boyfriend.

A-Ron: My *what?*

Charlotte: Well, he was over all the time. You liked to quilt.
And you had the pink gloves.

A-Ron: Those were yours! Razor threatened to *kill* me if I
didn't find a house and transplant the crop before the
snow fell. I transplanted an acre of marijuana by hand.
And I was locked inside your house with an angry,

paranoid biker for two months. You remember that time Mr. D knocked on the door to ask about the fish?

Charlotte: He said you had a dog.

A-Ron: The dog was the least of his worries. Razor was on the other side of the door with a sawed-off shotgun.

Charlotte: A gun?!

A-Ron: Razor was going to shoot him if he came inside.

Charlotte: Allan thought you were a bit rude.

A-Ron: I saved his life.

Charlotte: That was nice of you, dear.

A-Ron: Then a week after that I was in the bathroom when I heard someone kick in the front door. I heard Razor shout in pain. I heard him beg someone for mercy. I never in my life thought I would hear that sound.

I squished myself into the cupboard under the sink. For three hours all I could hear was bumping and crashing, I don't know what. Then nothing. I waited another hour. When I came out, everything was gone. All the plants, the lamps, everything. Gone.

And that's when I knew I was in too deep. Sorry about your house. I turned off the fan when I left. This is it for me, Mrs. Duncanson. Razor's gone, the pot has vanished. This is my chance to get out.

Pause.

Charlotte: Bullroar.

A-Ron: What?

Charlotte: Bullroar. That's what this is.

A-Ron: Mrs. Duncanson. I swear to God, I am telling the truth.

Charlotte: And you're an airline pilot too. And a gay. And you cook a mean stir-fry. How do I know any of it is the truth?

A-Ron: I guess — I guess you don't. Go ahead and press send.

Pause. Charlotte looks at the phone. She looks at Ron. She puts the phone away in her purse.

Charlotte: I'm not going to ruin your life for you. But if you want to ruin it, then you go right ahead and waste this opportunity. But you need to know that the next senior citizen might not be so forgiving.

A-Ron: Thank you, Mrs. Duncanson.

Charlotte: You can call me Charlotte.

A-Ron: Charlotte.

Ron leaves. Lights. In the condo.

Allan: I can't believe you let him go.

Charlotte: I can't believe you let Nesbitt off the hook.

Allan: It wasn't going to change anything to rake him over the coals.

Charlotte: And that's exactly why I let poor Ron go.

Allan: It's not the same thing.

Charlotte: It was still the Christian thing to do.

Allan: I'll tell you what the Christian thing to do is: an eye for an eye.

Charlotte: And soon the whole world is blind.

Allan: He single-handedly destroyed our home —

Charlotte: Not all by himself.

Allan: — you had him in the palm of your hand, *and you let him go.*

The phone rings. Allan wants to continue arguing, but he has to answer the phone.

Yep. Yep. Yep. See you in an hour.

Allan hangs up the phone.

Charlotte: *To Allan.* Who was that?

Allan: *Canada AM.* CTV. National television. Get your coat.

Charlotte: Why are we meeting *Canada AM*?

Allan: You remember Tina Vandenbilt's niece, don't you?

Charlotte: Sure. Nice girl. A bit heavy.

Allan: She went to Carleton for journalism school — they have one of them — what d'you call that — where they give you a job —

Charlotte: Placement?

Allan: So you can practice what you learned at school —

Charlotte: Practicum?

Allan: But they don't really pay you a full wage? Not volunteering, but —

Charlotte: Internship?

Allan: That's it! She's interning with this TV station. Come on.

Charlotte: Which one?

Allan: *Canada AM.* CTV. National television.

Charlotte: You're kidding!

Allan: No. They called last week. Seems marijuana is all the rage. *Canada AM* wants to do a story about grow operations.

Charlotte: We're going to be on national television!?

Allan: In an hour. I guess they want to show how the little guy gets hurt by all this.

Charlotte: *Flustered.* I'm going to have to get my hair done.

Allan: I'm sure they're going to be asking me a few questions. About the damage to the house. You know, the mould and all. About how much it's going to cost.

Charlotte: *Flustered.* Good lord, I haven't a thing to wear.

Allan: They'll probably ask about the insurance. What do you think I should say?

Charlotte blusters to the front of the stage, smoothing her blouse. A spotlight comes on her. She realizes that Allan is still behind her, in the previous scene. She rushes to get him and drags him into the spotlight.

The bright light of a TV camera shines in their faces. They are both incredibly camera-shy and a little too dumbstruck to put a complete sentence together. The best they can manage is reacting to the questions that we, the audience, do not hear.

Allan: Yep.

Charlotte: Uh-huh.

Allan: Sure.

Charlotte: Uh-huh.

Allan: That's about the size of it.

Charlotte: Uh-huh.

Allan: All over the walls here.

Charlotte: *Pointing.* Here.

Allan: The uh … the uh …. Dang, can't think of the word …

Charlotte: *Whispering.* Insurance.

Allan: Insurance! The insurance didn't come through.

Charlotte: *Shaking her head.* Uh-uh.

Allan: Bye now.

Charlotte: Uh-huh.

They pause. The light goes out. They immediately relax.

Charlotte: I've never been so embarrassed in all my life.

Allan: Oh, you did fine.

Charlotte: I couldn't say anything but "uh-huh." You made me look like an idiot.

Allan: Me?

Charlotte: You sprang this on me with no warning.

Charlotte stalks offstage, leaving Allan alone onstage. Allan is pacing, like he was at the beginning of Act One and Act Two: it is very recognizably the same moment in time.

Allan: So. That's how we got to where we are today.

Charlotte re-enters from offstage.

Charlotte: Waiting for that man and his environmental assessment. So we can either get on with our life...

Allan: Or die in debt.

Pause. Allan looks at his watch. He is nervous and anxious, like someone waiting for news which he is certain is going to be very, very bad.

Charlotte: Shouldn't be much longer.

Another, much longer pause. Allan sighs and looks down at the ground. He looks up and squints out at the raspberry patch.

Allan: This is where mother had her stroke. Right here, while she was picking raspberries for a pie. The stroke left her so weak she couldn't move. She was stuck. The road's right there, but no one could see her for the bushes, so here she was, stuck. When we found her, her hand was clutched tight around one of the branches. They had to cut the branch off to take her away.

Pause.

Charlotte, I don't want to die like that — stuck in the same place I've been all my life, too stubborn to let go.

Charlotte: I know.

Allan: I should have warned you. About the television. Sorry.

Charlotte: I'm sorry I let Ron go without talking to you.

Allan: *Reluctantly.* It was the right thing to do.

Pause. Allan and Charlotte hug. Or perhaps they are about to, but decide that hugging is too demonstrative for two people their age.

The **Inspector** *enters in a white jumpsuit wearing a gas mask.*[6] *His breath is loud, ominous. Allan and Charlotte turn to him.*

Allan: And? How bad is it?

Inspector: Mhuut dimall?

Allan: I think they might be.

Inspector: Mhmumm, Humm, gathhlodic hownt murphm.

Allan: You don't say.

Inspector: Thrdnjwu, jwisj.

Allan: So what you're really saying is —

Inspector: Mhmumm, goputhyl!

Allan: Well, that's —

Inspector: Humm, gathhlodic murphm.

Allan: Well, that's — that's just …

Inspector: Eggit, thrdnjwu, murhphnet, jwisj. Ficedsk.

Allan: … tickety-boo!

Allan hugs the Environmental Inspector. The Inspector flaps his arms wildly. Allan runs to the other side of the stage and executes an uncharacteristically enthusiastic pirouette. Lights.

Charlotte: What did he say?

Allan regains his composure.

Allan: Did you know the walls of our home are made out of plaster?

Charlotte: What else would they be made of?

Allan: Drywall. That's what the walls in every new house are made out of these days. But our house was built with old-fashioned plaster.

Charlotte: Don't keep me in suspense, Allan.

Allan: Have you ever seen a sheet of drywall left out in the rain? It just crumbles. Drywall is cheap and easy to use. But it's porous.

Charlotte: And plaster?

Allan: Resists moisture. All of that mould, covering all the walls in our entire house, it's all just sitting there on the surface. It will come right off with Lysol and a sponge. We might need to use a metal scraper, but that's the worst of it.

Charlotte: And it's —

Allan: Not toxic.

Charlotte lets out a long sigh of relief.

Charlotte: Lord love a duck.

Allan: It'll only take us a couple of days to clean it up. And then we're selling the house.

Charlotte: Allan …

Allan: Istvan called the other day. Seems Pishta is getting married and wants a house of his own.

Charlotte: But you were born here.

Allan: I was born in a hospital.

Charlotte: This farm has been in your family for one hundred and thirty-eight years.

Allan: My father bought it.

Charlotte: From his cousin.

Allan: His fifty-second cousin twice removed. Who he'd never even met. We're selling the house, Charlotte. The harder we try to hold onto the past, the more it turns on us. We're letting go. Starting now.

They hold each other, and gaze out at the audience.

Charlotte: I love this farm. Look out there. The fields and fields of crops, swaying in the gentle summer breeze.

Allan: The row of trees hugging the crick.

Charlotte: Another line of trees here, making a natural wind-break for the house.

Allan: The acre and a half of lawn, carved out of what used to be the old apple orchard.

Charlotte: This farm is in our blood.

Allan: But you can't hang on forever.

Charlotte: No matter how much you may want to.

They gaze out at the farm laid out before them. It's beautiful.

Allan: Say goodbye, Charlotte.

Charlotte: Goodbye, Charlotte.

THE END

ENDNOTES

1   Check real estate rates in your area for an accurate figure on the resale value of a middle-sized family farm in your region.

2   Due to Blyth's proximity to Toronto, this line and the sequence following did not work in the Blyth Festival production, and had to be amended as follows:

A-Ron: WestJet. "Six flights to **Calgary** every day."

Allan: Wouldn't think there'd be that many people that would want to go to **Calgary**.

C-Ron: Maybe they go to take in a game.

A-Ron: See the **Flames** win one.

and later ...

Charlotte: You have to stay overnight on a flight to **Calgary**?

A-Ron: ... I don't do **Calgary**. I do the **Florida** run.

Charlotte: And you have to stay over?

A-Ron: You can only fly so many hours at a time. Like truckers. Only more regulated.

Charlotte: It's just that ... **Florida** doesn't seem that far. I don't see why the airline makes you stay over.

3   We've tried this line with other regional groups: Mennonites in Blyth and Hutterites in BC. Feel free to try your own variation. The Blyth variation is below.

Policeman: Heck, I heard of some teenagers the other day down in **St. Jacob's** who were growing it in Grandpa's barn.

Allan: **Mennonites**?

Policeman: **Shunned Mennonites** now.

But keep in mind this is not a joke about religion, but about *region*. Southern Alberta, near Claresholm, is home to the largest population of Mormons in Canada; similarly, St. Jacob's is close to Mennonite country, so it would be natural for Allan to ask, in shock, if the culprits in question were members of that group. Ask yourself, as I did in both instances, if your Mormon or Mennonite friends would relish the joke or not.

4 In Ontario, some theatres like to change the line to "These days all insurance is run out of three or four big companies in Toronto" in order to make it work for their region. Lord knows what a theatre company in Toronto would have to change it to.

5 Of course, change the destinations of both the pick-up and the drop-off to suit your needs. In Blyth Ron picked up the bag in Windsor and dropped it off in Toronto. But it doesn't always need to be a big city: the Ft. McMurray reference worked at Lunchbox because the town had recently earned a reputation across the province for conspicuous drug consumption, due to all of the workers in the oil sands who were separated from family with money to burn and little to do in town.

6 OK, so I lied — there's three actors. Maybe it's an ASM or an intern or something. In the original one-act version Charlotte had time for a quick change offstage into a white suit with face mask; later she simply peeled the suit off while asking Allan what the man had said. This is still my favourite, as it preserves the challenge of using only two actors in all the parts, but when the play was expanded to two acts, a monologue was moved and this became difficult. The team in Blyth inventively asked the ASM to don a rubber glove and stick her arm onstage while the lines were delivered by a pre-recorded voice-over; the arm even got its own curtain call.

photo of Ken Cameron
by Sean Dennie

MY
MOROCCO

PLAYWRIGHT'S INTRODUCTION

My Morocco began life as a short story in early 2005 that was read at the Manitoba Association of Playwrights in Winnipeg, the Alberta Playwrights' Network's Auburn Cabaret (in Calgary) and the APN Littlefest Cabaret (in Edmonton). Full productions of this short version were performed with professional actors at Solo Collective in Vancouver and the Gateway Theatre in Edinburgh later that year. Though I was not lucky enough to see either in person, I knew instinctively that if I were to expand the story to include more of my relationship with my sister, then performing it myself would create a very different experience for the audience.

A full-length version of *My Morocco* was commissioned by Ghost River Theatre in the fall of 2005, with funding from the Alberta Foundation for the Arts, and was partially developed through Ghost River Theatre's Monday Night Storytelling class, led by Ghost River's founding artistic director, Doug Curtis.

Most of the play was written on a slow boat going down the Mekong River in the People's Democratic Republic of Laos. On that occasion, my now-wife Rita and I spent two uncomfortable days on a cramped riverboat next to an engine that precluded conversation. There was literally nothing to do but stare at the passing scenery and dream. As I dreamed, my thoughts turned to this half-finished play about my sister. Over the course of those two days, I was able to visualize the entire play so clearly that, when I returned to Canada, I felt as if I were simply transcribing a play that I had already fully composed.

The contribution of director Andy Curtis cannot be overrated, however. Andy and I, with the capable support of Assistant Director Dan Parry, trimmed and shaped the text to its current form. Andy was more than director and, really, more than dramaturg. Andy helped me to see what was important to the dramatic narrative and which details were obscuring the real issues that lay at the heart of the play. More importantly, since I had retired from acting thirteen years previous, Andy taught me how to act — or rather, how not to act and simply to be.

I also owe much to my then-fiancée and now-wife Rita Bozi and our stage manager, the mighty Ailsa Birnie, both of whom guided me through a six-week tour of the western Canadian Fringes and kept the performance honest and naked. Rita had her own opportunities to adjust the dialogue and coach the moments when I was playing her, and I am very proud to report that friends gave me credit for the accuracy of the portrayal. But more importantly, Rita gave me the title; she has since named all of my plays for me, since I am rarely happy with my working titles.

The casual nature of the performance, which I developed under the direction of Andy Curtis, is essential to the play. Two stories might illustrate this point. In developing the play, I performed it at several small cabarets, and each time I performed the first dozen pages or so (essentially the language lesson) extemporaneously, as if I were merely introducing the piece. Each time I returned to the podium as if to read, I thought of another bit of introduction I needed to make before I could begin. In this way, the beginning of the play bled seamlessly into our "real life." While we eventually discarded the device in the final performance, the sensibility of casual conversation and confession between performer and audience remained crucial.

The second discovery was made thanks to having several visitors in our rehearsal hall as part of an open rehearsal process. Andy urged me to make a specific connection with the audience and to refrain from simply delivering the text into a kind of middle space above the audience's head. I took this advice quite literally and borrowed a page from director Brian Quirt's production of *Through the Eyes,* making a point of looking each audience member in the eye throughout the production. This technique not only forced me to really, *really* speak to the audience, but it also forced me to be present, on this stage, in this moment, in a way that was eerily consistent with the themes of the play. Indeed, performing the play night after night became a kind of Buddhist exercise in being present.

Thanks to these wonderful mentors, I have discovered — or should I say, rediscovered — that the essence of acting is not putting on a face, but simply being present in front of an audience with a relaxed body and an open heart.

ACKNOWLEDGMENTS

These thanks must be reprinted in the program:

Special thanks to Rita Bozi (my consultant, spiritual guide, and soulmate), Allister and Carolyn Cameron, the Banff Centre for the Arts, the Alberta Playwrights' Network, the Solo Collective, Tara Blue, Adele Furness, Wauneta and Blue Collar Dance, Lindsay Burns, Stephen Schroeder, Doug Curtis, all those who contri-buted to the show's development … and of course, Beth.

PERFORMANCES

My Morocco premiered in a workshop production at the Oh Solo Mio Festival in London, Ontario in April 2006 in front of my entire family. I was terrified, but pleased they could be the first to hear the story. The play subsequently toured the Western Canadian Fringe circuit to Winnipeg, Saskatoon, and Edmonton in the summer of 2006.

PRODUCTION
Director: Andy Curtis *
Sound Designer: Peter Moller
Photographer: Rita Bozi
Assistant Director: Dan Perry
Stage Manager: Ailsa Birnie *
* courtesy of the Canadian Actors Equity Association

My Morocco received its Calgary premiere at the Big Secret Theatre April 4–14, 2007, as part of the Groundbreakers Series, produced by our fabulous supporters at the very generous Ground Zero Theatre in conjunction with One Yellow Rabbit Performance Theatre and The Desert Bus Company. This version was substantially redesigned by Terry Gunvordahl.

A NOTE ON PUNCTUATION/PERFORMANCE

My Morocco is intended to be performed as a one-man show, with a single actor playing all parts.

There seem to be three different ways of relating to the audience in this play, and I have tried to develop a method of formatting that makes this clear:

1   The actor is most often narrating, indicated by simple text. This is common, direct address. In this instance I have not named that character, as it is clearly the narrator.

2   The actor is sometimes playing both parts within a scene, and in these instances there is a fourth wall. I have tried to differentiate moments by indenting the dialogue and indicating who is speaking.

3   The actor is sometimes quoting another character while continuing to directly address the audience. To make matters more confusing for the performer, these three different states can bleed seamlessly from one to another, and it is not always possible to distinguish these moments on the page. It sounds more complicated than it is, but really it is the same technique we use unconsciously when telling a joke or relating a funny anecdote.

I have broken up the lines of dialogue into separate lines, not to emphasize the poetic nature of the text, but simply to indicate where natural rhythms and breath might fall. As the playwright was also the performer in the original production, these breaks were key to the writing process, and I have re-tained them here. Again, this formatting choice is not intended to lead the performer towards a heightened manner of speech; it is intended to facilitate natural speech.

A performer may wish to make his or her own choices in some instances, and not feel imprisoned by the way that I have formatted the text. I encourage actor and director to play around and explore the text.

MY MOROCCO

On the stage are a few music stands which face away from the audi-
ence. These music stands hold photos of Morocco printed onto stretched
canvas which are periodically revealed as the play progresses. (In a later
production, projections were used instead of manually revealing the
canvasses.) A few colourful Samsonite suitcases dot the stage.

Ken enters with more suitcases. He sets them down and greets the
audience.

"Salaam Alaikum." [1]

"Lebes?" [2]

"Hamdu'llah."

That's how you say hello in Arabic.
I learnt that when I was in Morocco.

Salaam Alaikum.
It means "Peace be upon you." Nice, eh?
I liked saying that a lot since 9-11,
since George Bush invaded Iraq,
since the Danish got in all that trouble for making fun
    of Mohammed.
since those 17 kids got arrested for trying to blow up
    Mississauga,

Peace be upon you.
"Salaam Alaikum."
Everyone say it with me — "Salaam Alaikum."

There, now you can say hello to a Muslim.
A very valuable skill in today's world.

Ken returns to the music stand and shuffles some papers around
as if we are about to finally begin.

Actually, that's not all there is to saying hello.
There is a whole ritual surrounding greetings in the Arab world.
At least in Morocco there is.

You are supposed to hug for one thing with your hand on your
   heart — and kiss on the cheek — both sides — which is not
   what we think of when we think of Muslims.
We think of Muslims shooting each other, not stopping in the
   street hugging and kissing each other — at least if you
   watch too much CNN like I used to, that's what you end
   up thinking.
Anyway, we hug and then I say "Salaam Alaikum."

Then you respond with "Walaikum assalam."
It means "And peace also be upon you."

Then I say, "La-bes?"
which means "Is everything OK?"
and then you respond with "La-bes."

Then I would say "Hamdu'llah" which means "Oh thank God."
I think technically it means "Allah be praised," right? Hamdu
   Allah? Hamdu'llah?
but they use it all the time, so colloquially it means "Thank God."
And then you guys would say "Hamdu'llah."
You have to say it like that, from the belly.
So let's try that.
I'll walk you throught it.
We meet in the middle of the street — say in Marrakesh —
   'you put your hand on your heart,
then we kiss on the cheek both sides.
I say "Salaam Alaikum,"
and then you guys say "Walaikum assalam."

The audience repeats, "Walaikum assalam."

Good. Then I say "La-bes" and you guys say "La-bes."

The audience repeats, "La-bes."

Good. Then I say "Hamdu'llah." Then you guys say "Hamdu'llah."

The audience repeats, "Hamdu'llah."

No, you have to say it from the belly.

The audience repeats, "Hamdu'llah."

Now you better not have anywhere pressing to be,
and in Morocco no one has anywhere pressing to be,
because now etiquette demands that you have to ask me about
    my whole family tree.

Let's give it a try — in English — to get the hang of it.

Ken picks a single audience member at random.

"You sir, how is your father, is he OK?"

The audience member responds with something along the lines of,
    "My father is fine thank you, how's yours?"

"And your mother how is she?"

The audience member responds with something along the lines of,
    "My Mother is fine thank you, how's yours?"

"And your brother how is he?"

The audience member responds with something along the lines of,
    "My brother is fine thank you, how's yours?"

"And your sister how is she?"

The audience member responds with something along the lines of
    "My sister is fine thank you, how's yours?"

Well, my sister... my sister ... I guess that's why I wanted to
    teach you a bit about how to say hello in Arabic.

It has to do with being in foreign territory.
It has to do with being in Morocco.

The call of the muezzin in the distance. The sound of waves lapping
against the shore. A soundscape that calls us to foreign lands ...

Hmm My Morocco ... the land of mosques
and minarets
Humphrey Bogart movies
Marrakesh Express
smelly toilets
cockroaches

Berber carpets
the Western Sahara
Paul Bowles and *The Sheltering Sky*
William S. Burroughs and *Naked Lunch*
The French Foreign Legion
Russell Crowe filmed the movie *Gladiator* in Morocco
Hannibal marched through with his elephants on his way to
    challenge Rome
the ground is so barren that goats climb trees to get anything
    to eat
women still wear the traditional black headscarves
they go swimming fully clothed
a man plays an oud while he's preparing my mint tea
olives
tagines
flat bread
glorious spices
right next to a garbage dump in the middle of the street
and lots and lots of interesting social politics.

My fiancée Rita and I were in Morocco visiting our friend
    Anthony, he teaches English as a second language.
I've taken to calling him Our Man in Casablanca,
because it makes me feel like a character in a Graham Greene
    spy novel.

So far Rita and I are about halfway through our two-week trip
    — we've been to Casablanca, Marrakesh, Essouria, and
    now Oulidia.

*Ken turns around the first of the music stands to reveal a photo
of Oulidia: beach, seagulls, and quaint fishing boats.*

Oulidia is a little town about 200 kilometres southwest of
    Casablanca along the Atlantic coast.
We're standing on a beach,
the sun is setting,
out there is the Atlantic Ocean,
over here is a tiny chocolate-bar-and-ice-cream kiosk,
and behind us a bank of public telephones.

The music stands become a bank of telephones. Ken tries first one,
then another. The phones do not seem to be working.

Ken: Hey!

Hey Anthony!

Yo!

Our Man in Casablanca, get your ass over here.

I can't make any of these stupid Moroccan telephones work.

Yes, I *have* to call them. They're my parents.

I've been here for a week already and I haven't phoned
home once.

I was going to call on Friday night, but it got pretty late

I was going to call them Saturday but we went to the beach

I was going to call them Sunday morning,

but we rented a boat and went to that little island on the
other side of the bay.

You know, I think I am avoiding calling my parents so that
I won't have to speak to my sister.

Don't any of these phones take change?

Yes, I have a phone card.

I bought it off some guy on the street in Marrakesh.

He said it was recycled?

I guessed it was illegal. I just hope it works.

I hate these cards.

They always say sixty credits, but what does that mean exactly?

How much is a credit?

Is one credit three minutes, is it thirty seconds, what exactly?

How do you dial these things?

You're always supposed to add a zero, or leave the zero off
in these foreign countries.

I always want to ask, "Why do you frickin' people have the
zero at all then?!"

Ken is about to hang up when:

Hello?

Pause. A moment of confusion.

Uh ... I'm looking for Allister and Carolyn Cameron.
Have
I got the right number?
This is their son Kenneth.
This is their son Kenneth!
Who's this?
Jean?
Listen, Jean, the credits are coming off this card faster
than the scarves off a two-bit Mata Hari in the Kasbah.
Can I speak to my parents?
Where are they?
They left you with a number?
I'm supposed to call them there?
Jean, has something happened to my parents?
You're not supposed to tell me?
It's not your responsibility?
Jean! I'm in Morocco.
I'm in Morocco!
Yes, it's very nice.
Jean, it's in Africa! I'm calling long distance and the
phone card is running out of money. Tell me what
happened Jean. Please.
No one's going to yell at you, I promise.
Just tell me what happened.

Pause.

My sister ....died ... of a heart attack?
Beth is dead?
What?
When?
Why?
Where's my Mom and Dad?
What funeral home? No, I don't have the number of the
funeral home, I'm in Morocco.
Give me the number. No wait, I don't even have a pen.
Anthony, get me a pen.
Thanks.
OK, Jean, go ahead. 519...

Well, why don't you get your glasses.

No! Jean! Don't put the phone down! I'm in Africa. I'm
    running—

To Anthony.

Getting her glasses.

I don't know she just —

Shh.

F***, it's beeping at me.

Gimme your card then.

In a panic, Ken puts the card in the phone.

It says… six credits. What does that mean six?

Come on Jean.

Come on.

Jean!

Yes, I'm here Jean.

519-762-84 — what?

8564.

Listen, Jean. You're sure that's a five? 8564?

OK.

Yes Jean, I think you did the right thing by telling me.

The phone dies. Ken hangs up. The call of the muezzin.

*   *   *

Here's the thing — when my sister died she and I hadn't spoken
    in two years.

Well, that's a bit of an exaggeration —

we'd spoken to each other,

just not politely.

We'd shouted at each other.

A lot.

Ken: **I'm never going to speak to you again!**

I suppose siblings all over the world make the same statement
    at some point in their lives — but no one ever expects it's
    going to turn out to be true.

* * *

I get the number for the funeral home just as the phone dies.
I need another phone card, but I left my wallet at the top of
    the hill.
So did Our Man in Casablanca.
We trudge up the hill in silence.
I have not got a single thought in my head.
You know how those Buddhist monks spend years meditating,
    trying to stop the incessant chatter of our monkey brains
    and achieve a higher state of consciousness in which the
    mind is emptied of everything except physical sensation?
It's kinda like that.

Actually, that's not true.
Not true at all.
About halfway up the hill, I have *one* thought.

"This would make a really great play."

I can't believe I'm thinking that.

Up at the top of the hill Rita is looking out at the lights of the
    fishing trawlers on the horizon.
Anthony slips quietly into the house.
I tell Rita my sister died of a heart attack.
I'm not crying.
My voice does not break or tremble.

If this were a play it would be much more dramatic.
That's the thing about theatre — you can make it better than
    real life.

* * *

*A weather report comes out of an old clock radio. It forecasts snow and
cold weather. Ken sighs and sits on the suitcases.*

Let's go back in time a few months,
Let's go back to a morning in early March.
I'm lying in my bed taking stock of the cold:
through the window I can see the big blue Alberta sky

that tells me that March has come in like a lion.
I feel a warm hand shaking my shoulder and I hear a giggle.
I moan and roll over.
Rita waves two airline tickets in my face and says:

Rita: I did something silly.

Ken: Rita, I can't afford a trip to Morocco now.

Rita: I knew you'd say no, so I made sure the tickets were non-refundable. My treat.

Ken: I don't want you paying for my vacation.

Rita: Then pay me back.

Ken: Rita, I can't afford to pay you back.

Rita: Oh, let's go!
You've been so grumpy lately.
We need to go somewhere exciting.

Ken: What I *need* is to write a new play.
I'm always kinda grumpy when I'm between projects.
I miss the thrill that I get when I create a whole new world from my imagination.
Now I'm between things.
I've run out of ideas.
And I'm worried.

Rita pulls out a journal with a Moroccan-style cover. She hands it to Ken.

Rita: Here. This is for your new play.
The one you're going to find in Morocco.

* * *

Back at the bottom of the hill I have my mother on the phone.
She tells me that Beth died of a very rare virus that attacked her heart.

Thursday morning.
Beth wakes up feeling sick to her stomach. Like she had food poisoning.

Must have been that tuna fish sandwich she had the night
   before.
She doesn't have to work today so she just goes back to bed.
But as the day wears on she's not feeling any better.
So she calls my Mom.
Mom leaps to the rescue.
She takes over some turkey soup from the freezer,
gives her some flat ginger ale, with no bubbles.
She tries dry toast but Beth just isn't feeling very hungry.

Beth just lies in bed watching her soaps and curled up with
   Barney, the dog.
There's nothing like curling up with a dog to make you feel
   better, huh?

Mom on the other hand is not one for sitting still.
So while Beth sleeps Mom mops the floors,
empties the cupboards,
washes the dishes,
puts the dishes back in the cupboard,
goes outside mows the lawn
rakes the grass
and weeds the flower beds.
Mom does this kind of stuff for Beth all the time,
she's over there at least once a week,
their lives are completely intertwined.

Nightfall: Beth still isn't feeling any better
so Mom figures she might as well just stay the night.
She asks Beth if she wants to go to the hospital but Beth says no.
It's just a bit of the flu;
who goes to the hospital for the flu?

Friday morning: Beth wakes up sweaty, out of breath and with
   an aching back.
Mom tells Beth,
"If you didn't smoke a pack a day, you wouldn't be out of
   breath.
Honestly, you're out of breath going up a flight of stairs."

So neither one of them even thinks twice about being out of
breath.

Beth takes a long shower, and that helps a bit, but by the time
she makes it back to bed
she's sweating all over again.

Five o'clock: Beth moves to the living room.
She puts Oprah on the living room TV, Barney curls up on
the couch next to her.
Her back is more sore than ever.

6:45: Beth begins to struggle for breath.

*Ken clutches his chest. For the briefest of moments, he becomes Beth,
unable to breathe. In an instant the vision is gone.*

All at once in a matter of seconds it is all she can do to manage short, sudden gasps, like someone hyperventilating.

*Ken clutches his chest, hyperventilating. He is again Beth, struggling
for breath. In an instant the vision is gone. These are the only two
moments of illustration in an otherwise plain-spoken and straightfor-
ward monologue.*

Mom helps her sit up.
"Put your head between your knees," she says.
"Try to catch your breath."
Beth's shirt is clinging to her back.

Mom looks in her daughter's eyes …
It's like looking at someone who knows they are drowning.
Mom goes to the phone.
"I need an ambulance to 264 Frances Street, Port Stanley."
Mom tries to remain calm.

Mom goes back to the couch, she puts some pillows behind
Beth's back.
She pushes Barney off the couch.
Mom tries to breathe in time with her, tries to help Beth get
control of her breah.
Beth's forehead is cold and clammy, just like when she had
the croup.

Mom looks outside the patio window, hoping to see the
ambulance.
There aren't even any cars on the street outside that she can
flag down.
And in Ontario, Port Stanley is a long way from London.
How long will an ambulance take?

Mom picks up the phone again.
Maybe she was too calm when she called before,
maybe she should have panicked,
maybe the operator couldn't tell from her voice how bad it
really was.
Mom tells them to send a fire truck,
there's a fire department in town,
they'll know what to do.
The operator says,
"That's what we're doing, ma'am,
the truck has already left,
they'll be there any minute."

Mom sets down the phone and by the time she makes it back
to the couch Beth is no longer breathing.
Mom rushes behind the couch and starts mouth-to-mouth
resuscitation.
But my mother took that St. John's Ambulance course back
in 1977,
she's not sure if she's creating a clear passageway,
she doesn't know if any air is getting through,
she doesn't even know if she's doing it right.

Mom gives her daughter five, maybe seven, breaths
when the fire truck pulls up the drive.
The firemen are all volunteers.
They're friends and neighbours
people who know Beth from the grocery store, the post office,
the beach.
But they have training, they know what to do,
they drag Beth off the couch and lay her on the floor,
they have started CPR before that truck has even stopped moving.

Mom stays out of the way.
She leans against the cool glass of the patio window.
Barney is curled up nervously at her feet.
The Simpsons are on TV.
The antique clock,
the one that our grandfather had refurnished and which
    Beth kept on the mantelpiece strikes seven o'clock.

Thirty-six hours after the onset of the first symptoms, fifteen
    minutes after Beth started struggling for breath, and she
    was dead.

The coroner said later that even if Mom had taken Beth to
    the hospital on Thursday morning
even if the doctors had figured out it was her heart that was
    the problem
the only thing they could have done was a complete heart
    transplant within 24 hours.
And there's a waiting list for that.

A clock strikes seven times.

* * *

Boy, what a great play this would make, huh?
It has dramatic potential.
The stakes are really high.
It is set in an exotic locale.
It could be a simple solo show,
a couple of suitcases,
an honest connection with the audience.

I can't believe I'm even *thinking* about making a play out of my
    sister's death.
I only found out yesterday.
It's so mercenary.
It's selfish,
I'm such an asshole.

There would have to be flashbacks of course.
That's where we would find out more about Beth ...

That's how we would learn about the roots of the conflict
between brother and sister ...

* * *

Ken addresses Beth.

Ken: Look, Beth, this really sucks.
When you call my house, you don't even say hello to Rita,
you act like you don't even know her.
You hate her and this is your way of letting her know it.
And I'm left trying to mediate between my sister and the
woman I love
neither of whom will speak to each other.
It's killing me.

Beth addresses Ken.

Beth: I hate her because I love you.
I'm just trying to protect you.
Kenneth, you were in another relationship, you were
practically married.
Well, maybe you should have tried another counselor.
No, she doesn't remind me of my divorce.
Well, maybe a little bit.
I don't want to have to make you choose between your
sister and your girlfriend, because if I try to make you
choose then I am just going to lose.

I have so tried.
Well ... I gave her presents at Christmas.
I had no money and I went into debt to give her —
And she sneered —
She did so. She sneered at them.
Well, no one told *me* she didn't want presents.
See, she doesn't want presents, so she doesn't want to be
part of the family.

Ken addresses Beth.

Ken: Goddammit, Beth. You knew I was out of town and you
called my house at two o'clock in the morning.

And the things you said.
It was like harassment.
I wouldn't let a complete stranger speak to Rita that way
   and I am sure as hell not going to let you.
You said it yourself:
if you are going to try to make me choose between my
   sister and my girlfriend
then you are going to lose.

I am never going to speak to you again.

* * *

*The sound of an ancient diesel bus sputtering to a start and slowly
wheezing down the road.*

We were up at dawn to catch a bus back to Casablanca.
I hardly slept a wink all night, or if I did it sure doesn't feel like it.
Anthony's cellphone rings while we're still on the bus.

Anthony: Hello? Ken, I think it's your dad.

Ken: Dad?

Dad: Hello?

*Ken's dad speaks loudly into the phone. Ken pulls the phone away
from his ear.*

Yeah that's my dad, all right.

Ken: Hi, Dad?

Dad: I'm looking for Kenneth Cameron.

Ken: Dad, it's me! Can you hear me!?

Dad: Kenneth?

Ken: What time is it there?

Dad: What?

Ken: What time —

Dad: Two o'clock in the morning.

Ken: It's two o'clock in the morning. Dad, what are you doing calling so early?

Dad: You said there was— Hold on. *To Carolyn.* Carolyn! Carolyn! He said there was six hours difference? *To Ken.* Yeah, son, you said there was six hours difference. Isn't that —

Ken: Dad, you're supposed to *add* six hours.

Dad: *To Carolyn.* Carolyn! You were supposed to add six hours.

Ken: Dad —

Dad: Kenneth —

Ken: Dad —

Dad: Kenneth —

Ken: Dad —

Dad: Kenneth —

Ken: Dad! There's a delay on the line, so we keep stepping on each other's sentences. Let's talk like we're in the military. Over.

Dad: Why?

Ken: Because —Just humour me. OK? Over.

Dad: Your mother and I don't think you should come home. It will be too expensive.... Over.

To Carolyn. We're pretending we are in the military. Don't ask.

Ken: I can put it on my Visa. I haven't had the chance to talk to the travel agent yet. Over.

Dad: Roger that, but there's no point. The last day of the visitation is today. Over.

Ken: What do you mean the last day? Dad? Over.

Dad: We had no way to find you. We had no contact number. You should have given us this kid's cellphone number before you left. Your mother even had our MP call the Canadian embassy and we still couldn't get a hold of you. Over.

Ken: Maybe I can have my own visitation. Over.

Dad: The body is going to be cremated tomorrow. Over.

Ken: Tomorrow?

Dad: You can't just leave a body lying around indefinitely. Not in summer. There's a time limit for this sort of thing. We can have a memorial service when you get back. Over.

Ken: I — I still — I'll come home and be with you. Over.

Dad: We're supposed be in Ireland next week, for the family reunion. The minister says we might as well still go. He says we can mourn in Ireland just as easily as we can grieve in Canada. Besides, we wouldn't want to waste the tickets. Your Aunt Charlotte and Uncle Don are going too, so we'll be surrounded by family —

Ken: *To himself.* Well, not all your family.

Dad: How's August? For the memorial service? Over.

Ken: *To himself.* You mean … I have to mourn by myself for the next six weeks?

Dad: Kenneth? We thought August would be kinda nice, close to Beth's birthday. Might give you time to write a eulogy. Over. Can you hear me? Over.

Ken: Eulogy? Uh … Yeah, no problem. How was the visitation? Were there many people? Over.

Dad: We had over two hundred people last night. All her figure skating students came, with their families, they drove over two hours to get here. They were lined up around the block. The funeral home stayed open two

hours late to make sure everyone got in. We might have
as many again tonight. Maybe more. Over.

Ken: Over.

Dad: Over.

Ken: Over.

* * *

An airplane takes off. Music.

Lesley: Ken? It's Leslie, your travel agent.
I'm so sorry to hear about your sister.
Now I can't get you back to Canada any earlier than the flight
you are already on, which leaves next Sunday at 12:05.
But I can get you to Ireland.
You take the first leg of your regular flight,
from Casablanca to Frankfurt-au-Main using Royal Moroccan
Air.
You see Rita off on her flight back to Calgary.
Meanwhile, you change terminals,
exchange your Air Canada ticket for Belgium Air
and fly to London, Heathrow.
At Heathrow you get to change terminals again,
and take an Aer Lingus flight to Dublin.
You spend five days with your parents,
(well, four and a half really)
and at the end of that week you take the bus with them and
the family reunion tour group all the way up to Belfast.
There's no room left on their charter flight back to Canada,
so when they go to the airport, you take a ferry from Belfast
to Glasgow.
From Glasgow you fly to Toronto
where you only have to wait six hours at the airport before
carrying on to Calgary...
via Thunder Bay.
And Winnipeg.
And Saskatoon.

And the best part is, all of this is on bereavement fare,
so it's only going to cost you twenty-five hundred dollars.

I don't have twenty-five hundred bucks; I could put it on my Visa,
but Mom and Dad said I shouldn't even bother.

Dad: "Don't worry about us — we'll be surrounded by family."

* * *

The call of the muezzin.

Ken: Oh geez, that fricking call to prayer. It's right outside our
      window.
      It's five o'clock in the morning.
      Hey, Rita, are you awake?
      Rita?
      I had this horrible dream that Beth died of a heart attack
          and ...
      Oh.
      That's like getting the news all over again.

      Man, it's only five in the morning and already it's stinking hot.

      I'm having trouble picturing Beth clearly.
      I can't see her face.
      I can't hear her voice.
      My memory of her is evaporating.
      I'm in shock. That's all.

      I wish I had a picture of her in my wallet.
      I don't even have a picture of you with me.

      If I was at home I'd just get out the ...
      I don't even have a picture of Beth in our home.

The call of the muezzin. He closes his eyes again.

      Maybe if I just concentrate more ...
      Focus.

The call of the muezzin. He closes his eyes and tries harder.

Beth is wearing sandals on the Columbia Icefield,
because where she lives it's still summer
and no one ever told her that a glacier would be colder
   than the beach.
She's wearing my jacket
it's way too big for her
and we're all laughing at how silly she looks.
The best part is she's laughing hardest of all.

Every time I hear the call to prayer — five times a day —
I will stop whatever I am doing,
even if I am in the middle of the street,
and I will make a point of picturing Beth's face.
By the end of the week, I can have pictured her face
   twenty-five times.

* * *

And now the five stages of grief.

Ken: Anger
      Anger
      Anger
      Anger
      Anger

      Anger anger anger anger anger anger

* * *

A crescendo of sound. The sound transports us to a hotel room.
He looks around.

Ken: Tangier. Shit.

Rita: Look at this room! I love these tiles.

Ken wearily drags the suitcases into the room.

Rita: Ken! No don't put the suitcases on the bed!
       You'll get the bedspread all dirty.
       No don't put them there you'll block the bathroom.

Ken: Fine!

Ken drops the suitcase onto the floor. Something breaks. Silence.

Rita: Was that the mirror we bought for our bathroom?

Ken: *Muttering.* Sorry.

Rita: It was one of a kind.

Ken: I said I was sorry, for Christ's sake.
    Rita don't open the shutters.
    I can't stand the sun.

Ken turns around one of the music stands to reveal a window with shutters. Rita tries to cheer Ken up.

Rita: *Cheerily.* The guidebook said this was the hotel where
    William S. Burroughs wrote the novel *Naked Lunch.*
    In room number nine, it says, but there is no room number
        nine.
    It only goes to eight. And this is room number eight.
    So maybe it was this room.

Rita reaches out and runs her hand across the black lacquer of the desk.

    Maybe he set up his Underwood typewriter right here
        on this table.
    Maybe he sat in that chair,
    shot up with heroin,
    then typed out all that weird stream-of-consciousness
        hallucinatory BS about his typewriter turning into
        a cockroach.

Ken: When you first told me that we were going to Tangier,
    this was one of the only things I wanted to do.
    Now that I'm here, I'm too screwed up to enjoy it.

Rita: The guidebook says all the famous Beat poets stayed here
    at one time or another:
    Burroughs, Kerouac, Ginsberg.
    Apparently there are photos in the bar downstairs.
    You want to go the bar?

Ken: My sister died three days ago.

Rita: And walking around like a zombie is not going to change
    that!
    Yesterday you nearly walked into traffic.

Ken: I did?

Rita: Ken. You have to be present, in this moment right here.

Ken: It's my parents that I feel most sorry for.
    No parent should live to see their child in a coffin.

Rita: "Should," where does that "should" come from?
    Where is that written? In what book?
    It's your belief that says that parents shouldn't outlive
        their children.
    But the universe doesn't follow "should"s or "must"s or
        "have to"s.
    The universe does what the universe does,
    and trying to change what the universe does,
    trying to change what "is,"
    that's the beginning of suffering.
    Your sister is dead.
    I'm sorry but you can't change that, you can only observe it,
        "be" with it.
    You want to change what "is."
    You are in Morocco, so you try to not be in Morocco,
        running to internet cafés,
    yelling at computers that don't work,
    trying to call back to Canada on phones that don't want
        to connect.
    Try connecting with this moment, right here.

Ken: Don't give me all that Buddhist bullshit!
    Sarcastically. Being in the moment!
    I don't like this moment, thank you very much, and I don't
        particularly want to "be" in it.
    Oh God. I'm so alone.
    Someday my parents will die and now that Beth is gone,
    I will be all alone in this world.
    I will have no family.

Rita: You'll have no family? That really hurts.
    What about me?
    What about us?
    You're not grieving.
    You are trapped in your own drama
    and until you decide to stop being a character in your own
        story
    you can't be the author of your own fate.

Ken: That's really great philosophy,
    but abstract theoretical thinking about the nature of an
        essentially hostile universe and its relationship to a
        man without God
    is not what I need right now.

Rita: That's not what I said.

Ken: What I need right now is a little bit of sympathy.
    A hug maybe.

Rita: The idea of hugging someone who yesterday
    blamed me for keeping him away from his sister
    is not particularly appealing to me right now.

Ken: And the idea of marrying a woman who can't give me a
    hug when I need it is not particularly appealing either.

Rita: Well ... there it is then.

Ken: Well, there it is.

                    * * *

Ken crosses to a music stand, as if he is about to give a lecture.

Whenever I travel abroad I always try to take in a little bit of
    theatre so I can write off the whole trip against my taxes.
But in Morocco there is no theatre.
And no visual representation through painting or sculpture in
    the traditional European post-Renaissance manner either,
    in case you were wondering.
You see, Allah created the world.

He separated the land from the sea,
he created the birds and the fishes,
the mammals and the insects,
he created man and woman,
he created life … and death.

How dare you reproduce Allah's greatest creation?

And as the Danish found out to their horror,
making a caricature of Allah's greatest prophet is really, really
    bad.
But the thing is, it's not just that they made fun of Mohammed.
It's that they made a picture of him at all.

Consequently, Moroccan religious and public art follows a
        much more abstract and decorative path and has perfected
        the use of endless interlaced geometrical motifs.
This is why they are so good at rugs.

As a principle of religion, it kind of makes sense to me.

How can you embrace the world that God has created if you
        spend all your time trying to replicate it, to improve upon
        it, to reframe it, to control it?
It's kinda like being that guy that always looks at all the plaques
        on the side of the road and completely forgets
        to look at the mountain vista right in front of him.

It's like that riddle.

*Turning around one of the music stands, Ken reveals a picture of
a window.*

"This is not a window."
"Well, what is it then?" Anyone?
"It's a painting of a window."
Actually, it's not even a painting of a window, it's a photograph
        of a window. See?
It's just made to look like a painting 'cause it's printed on canvas.
Nothing is real, but everything is true.
Everything is representation.

Even this play.

We're not really in Morocco; this is a representation of Morocco.

These aren't really emotions that I'm feeling; they are represen-
tations of emotions.

Rita keeps saying to me:

Rita: Do you think that if you channel your feelings into a play
then you won't have to actually feel your emotions?
Is that why you're holding on?

* * *

I tell Rita, I haven't taken a poo in four days.

Most people when they travel outside of North America or
Europe will,
at one time or another,
experience a little bit of a problem with *diarrhea*.
Me, I have the opposite thing going on.
I'm a keeper.

Rita says:

Rita: Our physical issues are a manifestation of our emotions
and our beliefs.
Our beliefs dictate how we react to the world.
You're reacting by clenching, holding on.
It's a sign you need to loosen up.

I say: Either that or it's a sign I need to eat more fruit.

Rita: Every body part, every endocrine, every organ has a
consciousness.
I have this book on the bowels you should read: it's called
The Second Brain.
Your colon knows that you are holding onto something,
and so your conscious colon is emulating you.
What is it you are holding onto?

Ken: My feces.

She doesn't speak to me for an hour.

Rita and I have traveled to Chefchaouen³, high in the Rif
   mountains.

I'd have preferred to stay in Tangier, or even Casablanca —
heck, I'd have preferred to go home —
but Rita says if I can't get *out* of here, I might as well *be* here.
She's traveling through Morocco;
I'm traveling through a fog.

Ken clutches his chest and breathes deeply in the sweltering heat.

It was supposed to be cooler in the mountains, but there's a
   record heat wave.
It's hotter than anyone can remember.
We decide that it has to be cooler in the Kasbah,
because a Kasbah is basically a big stone castle.
We are just about to pass through the main gate
when we are accosted by a big bald guy in a fez.

Ibrahim: English, are you English?

Ken: Uh …. No …. Ukraine …

Ibrahim: Ah, Ukraine! Vriady-hody.
   Huh?
   No Ukraine. Where from?
   Canada! I have friend in Montreal!!
   Calgary?
   Um …. Ah—ha! Stampede! Greatest Outdoor Show on
      the Earth!
   I know you have plans, but … every delay lead to the
      unexpected.
   Come.
   Spend time with me in my carpet shop.
   You will not be disappointed.

And Rita says "yes."

Ken: Rita, we're supposed to be going to the Kasbah.
   Remember? Rock the Kasbah? It closes at four.
   Maybe, for once, we could just do the thing we set out to
      do in the first place?

Rita: You're such a keeper. It might be a nice out-of-the-way
     place.

Ken: True. It also might be a narrow dead-end alley where
     he beats the shit out of me, rapes you, and takes all
     our money. We just don't know, do we?
     Where are you going?
     Rita!
     Rita!

So, we're shopping for carpets.
The bald guy is named Abraham.

Ibrahim: *Ibrahim.*
     Grandfather of Jacob who took the name Israel
     and became the father of the Jews
     and of Esau who became the father of the Arabs.
     Is it not interesting that the Jews and the Arabs come
     from the same family?

Ibrahim turns to Rita.

Ibrahim: This your husband?
     So handsome.
     And you, so beautiful.
     Canadiennes, always so beautiful,
     always such pleasure to have Canadiennes in my shop.

Ibrahim pulls a carpet out of one of the suitcases.

Ibrahim: This is Berber carpet. I am Berber. My mother Arab,
     my father Berber. You see? Flat-weave. *Kilim.* Very simple.

He lays the carpet on the ground.

     Zigzag design. Diamond design. Very nice. Elegant.
     You! Boy!
     Do you like mint tea?
     No sugar? But you must have.
     No? Very well.
     You! Boy! Mint tea! Sans sucre! Vite!
     Look at you. So beautiful.

You lucky man. Lucky, lucky, lucky man!
And him so handsome. You both, together, so beautiful.

He lays another the carpet on the ground.

This Rabat carpet.
Very thick.
Very good quality.
Good for special room.
But more expensive.
No? Very well.

He lays another the carpet on the ground.

This use vegetable dye, all natural.
Organic.
Chemical dye, very bad. Fade very fast.
Look!
Look at this colour.
This colour is *aphrodisiac*.
Good for jiggy jiggy.

I've got to get out of here.
I need to get some air.
I need to go back to the hotel.
No — no — I need to go *home*.
My guts are roiling.
I'm all cramped.
I need to move.
I need to stretch.
I need — I need to poo.

Ken: Rita, let's get out of here.

Ibrahim: You need bathroom?
I have bathroom!
Upstairs.
And also bucket, for washing hands.
Please.

Ken: Right. Rita, just don't buy anything while I'm gone, OK?

Ken creeps his way upstairs.

Upstairs, there is no second floor to Ibrahim's shop, there is
    only roof.
In front of me is a small sink, with a washboard,
and to the right a single clothesline, with a few sad articles of
    clothing baking in the sun
a T-shirt, a pair of pants, three socks;
likely all the clothing that Ibrahim owns in the whole world.

Ken sniffs the air.

I can smell it before I can see it.
At the other end of the roof is a small shack about the size
    and shape of an outhouse.

Now, I've smelled some smells during my time in Morocco.
You can't avoid it.
Just walking down the street in Morocco means alternating
    between some of the most glorious smells you have ever
    come across ... and some of the worst putrescence.
More glorious smells, more putrescence, more glorious smells,
    more putrescence...
But this.

There's no door.
Inside, there's a flat ceramic thing,
in the centre, a small hole, on either side of the hole, two
    ceramic foot treads.

Ken squats.

I just look out the door.
Bare mountains, covered in scrub and rock.
The heat wave searing anything green that might be trying to
    cling to the ground.
Chefchaouen.
Used to be part of the infamous Hippie Trail.
Apparently you still can't go for a walk in the hills without
    someone appearing from behind a shrub trying to sell
    you a brick of hash.

Or kif as it's called here.
There are a couple of minarets nearby.

I glance around. There is a cockroach on the wall about the
    size of a baby's fist.
I blow on it
its wings open
it takes off
pegs me in the head
falls to the floor beside ... a toad?
There's a toad in my stall.
A toad so perfectly camouflaged that I didn't even see it.
The toad scoops up the cockroach with its tongue
little cockroach legs struggling in the air for an instant before:
gulp.

The sound of the muezzin. Ken sighs. Not the most opportune time,
but a promise is a promise ...

Beth taught me how to smoke when I was ten.
We were on vacation in Florida.
She and her friend thought it was funny.
I thought her friend was beautiful.
Later that summer Beth was driving me to swimming lessons;
we were driving a little too fast on the gravel road, we came
    over a rise, the road went right,
and we didn't.
The first thing Beth did was make sure I was all right.
Then she checked the car.

Beth: "You're not going to tell mom and dad, are you?"

Ken: "Not if you give me a cigarette then I won't tell anybody."

Pause. Ken glances around.

No toilet paper.
There is a bucket, beneath a small tap.
Truth is, I don't need it.
I'm still holding on.

Rita: Ken, Look at the carpet I bought!
   Isn't it beautiful?
   I know, I know, but we said we might try to buy a carpet
      for our wedding. Remember?
   And guess what day it is?
   It's July 23.
   One year, exactly, from today and we'll spread this out on
      the grass at our wedding and say our vows.

Ibrahim: You get married?
   Wonderful!
   Tonight we celebrate!
   My house, you come!

As far as I am concerned,
It's not a good idea to go to a stranger's house when you are
   in a foreign country
and no one knows where you are.
But I was outvoted, one to one.
I wrote Ibrahim's name and address out on a little piece of paper
and left it on the bed,
so that if we don't come back
the police will know where to start looking for our bodies.

Ibrahim: My beautiful Canadiennes!
   I love you!
   Some days I no make sale.
   No sale, no money — no money, no eat.
   But today, I make sale.
   To you.
   I love you!
   So today, I eat.
   I eat, we eat.
   Hamdu'llah.
   Look!
   Olives, bread, wine.
   Welcome to my home.

   Yes, it is small, but Insha'llah.

You know this word?
Insha'llah?
It mean, "god willing."
Yes? *Insha …Allah? Insha'llah.*
It is, how you say … all-purpose.
It mean, "Ah, maybe yes, maybe no."
You ask, "You come over to my house for dinner?"
I say, "Yes … Insha'llah."
You say, "Pay me the money you owe me next week." I say,
"Yes … Insha'llah."

Ken: So … Basically it's a way of abdicating your responsibility
by saying that the matter in question is in the hands
of Allah, and thus, you have no control over it, thus it
is not your responsibility.

Ibrahim: You understand Insha'llah!
But Insha'llah is also bad.
Many people do nothing,
are lazy,
Say instead Insha'llah.
But Allah does not help the man who sits down in front
of moving bus.
You want to smoke some kif?

Ken: Rita, I'm not sure this is such a good idea.
We should stay on our guard.

Rita: Ken is sad because his sister died.

Ibrahim: SIDA?

SIDA? What does he mean SIDA?
Oh, SIDA is French for AIDS.
No wonder he's asking about AIDS…
This is Africa.

Ken: No.
My sister died of a heart attack.
She was only forty-one.

Ibrahim: Forty-one? Too young.
   My father have heart attack but he very old.
   I have sister and mother.
   I leave school.
   I join army.
   In Western Sahara.
   You know Western Sahara?
   Long ago was Spain.
   Spain leave, Morocco move in.

   Army do many bad things in Western Sahara.
   Many things, I do not like.
   So, I do not do these things.
   So, I go to jail.
   Not plain jail.
   Royal Moroccan Army jail.
   Five years.
   Ken, you look tense — You want massage? I learn massage
      in jail.

Before I know it he's got me flipped over onto my stomach.
And Rita's just laughing.

Ibrahim: You beautiful boy.
   Small.
   Nice.
   Feel good?

I have a large, sweaty, bald man who has just admitted that he
   was kicked out of the army and thrown in jail stroking my
   back.

Ken: Yeah, sure… feels great.

Ibrahim: Ken, you are tense.
   I will help you relax.
   Beautiful boy.
   Small.
   Nice.

I think I was starting to understand what Ibrahim learned in jail.

I'm starting to feel like a character in a William S. Burroughs
novel.

Ibrahim: Ken, relax.

> In Morocco, everyone go to mosque, everyone love the
> King, everyone say same thing.
> But how they feel, what they think — this never they say.
> Is Canada like this?
> Everyone hide feelings?
> Tsk, tsk, tsk, bad for heart.
> Feeling, feeling deep, is good for heart.
> Sit up.
> All done, my beautiful boy.
> Never hide feeling!!!
> Promise, Ken?
> Promise to live with open heart?
> You are both so beautiful.
> I will love you forever.

* * *

The call of the muezzin.

Ken: My sister got a friend of hers to take us both sailing once.

> I had just gotten my new job six weeks before
> and as the boat pulled away from shore
> I panicked.
> The little voice inside of me said:
> "What am I doing?
> I have so much work to do.
> There are all these people who are depending on me
> I have to call them all back,
> I have to save the world one play at a time."
> But the boat was well out of the harbour,
> I was trapped.
>
> Beth sat down beside me
> and handed me a beer.
> She put her hand on my knee and said:

Beth: Ken, you are my brother and I will love you forever.
　　But you can't be like this:
　　You'll have a heart attack before you're forty.

*   *   *

Ken falls asleep. Lights fade to the blue nighttime. A sudden, insistent knocking at the window. Ken wakes up.

Ken: Beth? ... Beth? ... Beth?!

Pause. He realizes.

　　Oh.
　　What was that knocking?

I cross to the window and throw open the shutters.

Outside on the patio, there is a tall, thin, old man in a dirty
　　undershirt and a battered brown fedora looking up at
　　the stars.

Ken becomes Burroughs, wearing the battered fedora.

Ken: Are you ...?

Burroughs: William S. Burroughs. At your service, shithead.

Ken: Wow... how did you get here?

Burroughs: There's no line between the "real world" and the
　　world of myth and symbol, kiddo.
　　In this half-life of ours, objects, sensations hit with the
　　impact of hallucination.
　　I am as real as the ground you're standing on, and as
　　ephemeral as the emotions you're feeling.

Ken: What is that noise?

Burroughs: Oh, that's just Ginsberg.
　　He's practicing the harmonium.
　　Allan!
　　Knock it off.
　　And put some clothes on, you're scaring the children.

Now, listen up, 'cause there's nothing I hate more than
   having to repeat myself to morons.
No one can cheat death, but that's not necessarily a bad thing.
Man is an artifact designed for space travel.
He is not designed to remain in his present biologic state
   any more than a tadpole is designed to remain a tadpole,
or any more than a cockroach is designed to remain ...
whatever the hell a cockroach is before it becomes a
   cockroach.

Ken: So ... there is life after death.

Burroughs: How the hell should I know?
   I'm not an angel, I'm a figment of your imagination.
   And a worn-out junkie to boot.
   All I know is that when you become death, death is the
      seed from which you grow.
   The Muslim knows this:
   he believes that death is the return of the soul to its
      creator.
   The whole of what we call life is merely a giant test,
   like an SAT for eternity.
   What matters to the Mohammedan is not that his life will
      come to an abrupt end;
   but whether his SAT scores are good enough to get him
      into Allah U.
   So there's no point in taking any of this absurdity too
      seriously.

Ken: Uh, OK. Thanks.

Ken turns to go. He pauses, and turns back.

   Just one last question Mr. Burroughs.
   What is *Naked Lunch* about?

Burroughs: No idea.
   I know I'm some kind of interplanetary agent
   but I don't think my signals are decoding properly.
   Who gives a shit anyway?
   It was just a book, it's not like I made it my life.

What about you kid; did you live your life today?
Or did you just write about it as it went by?
Now fuck off and let me enjoy the moonlight.

* * *

In the morning I tell Rita I need some time to myself.
She's kind of upset.
There isn't much that a single woman can do in Morocco by
    herself.
I don't care.
I head out of the medina and make for the city gates.
It's surprising how small this town really is.
It's not long before I'm well into the wilderness, the pristine
    whitewashed walls of the city receding behind me.
The rumours aren't true, there's no one around to sell me a
    brick of hash.

I sit down on a rock, the sun beating down on my head.

Ken pulls out the journal.

Ever since I was ten, eleven years old, I've carried a little book
    like this.
Now it's time to polish Beth's eulogy.

He opens the journal and begins to write.

Ugh, I sound like a preacher. I can do better than that...
No ... no, too repetitive.
"loved by her family, *admired* by her students, *honoured* by her
    friends."
Good.
That'll get 'em.
"Her life was tragically cut short —"
What a cliché.
But clichés work, that's how they become clichés.
" — and her death has touched us all."

This is good, it's well-written, it will really grab people,
it will make everyone cry,
but there isn't one authentic feeling in any of this drivel.

It's all illusion.

How can you embrace the world that God has given you if you
   spend all your time trying to create a world of your own?

A bus rattles up the road towards the city, stops and an old
   man gets out.

The bus pulls away towards the city,

the old man heads in the opposite direction, up into the hills.

Ken: There's nothing up there. That's the middle of nowhere.

I mean *literally* the middle of nowhere.

It's a desert mountain.

Red rubble like the surface of Mars and as hot as Satan's
   bedchamber.

Nothing in sight.

No farms. No houses. No huts. No trees. No nothing.

Look at him, he's walking determinedly up a stairway to the
   blazing African sun.

Hmm.

This is the *African* sun.

This is the sun they always write about.

This is the sun of Egypt and of Libya of the Sahara ... and of
   Darfur.

This sun is foreign to my pale Canadian skin.

This is *not* the same sun that shines down on my poor parents
   as they stand next to my sister's coffin back in Canada.

That is a whole different sun, a cold North American sun,
   that greets their grief this day.

Pulls out notebook.

"I feel ... lonely ..."

Is that the call to prayer?

It must be about time.

Focus.

Not on a memory this time, but on an emotion.

Any authentic feeling.

Any feeling.

*Long pause. Ken tries to focus on a feeling, but he finds only empti-
ness inside. He squeezes his eyes tight, and tries harder. Again, there is
nothing but an empty void inside. In silence he pounds his stomach, or
his leg, anything to try to find a feeling ... any feeling. He emits a cry
of frustration and tears. Silence. The life drains from his limbs. Slowly
he opens his eyes.*

It's like trying to squeeze tears out of this pebble on the
    ground.

What if Moroccans are right?
What if every time you use an emotion in a work of art,
you give away a little piece of your soul?
What if every time you cry onstage,
that's one less time you can cry in real life?

*   *   *

*Music: aggressive Moroccan drumming, a driving rhythm that seems
to raise the blood pressure just listening to it. Ken puts the suitcases
side by side to simulate seats on a bus with an aisle down the centre;
he sits on one of the suitcases.*

Rita and I have made the classic airline traveler's mistake:
You'd think we'd have figured out by now that a plane that
    leaves at 12:05 AM on Sunday means just that:
Five minutes after midnight in the wee hours of Sunday
    morning.
But no, we've lost a whole 24 hours all because we misunder-
    stood our ticket.

Now we have to get up at an ungodly early hour on Saturday
    morning,
endure a six-hour bus ride back into Casablanca,

pick up the remainder of our belongings from Anthony's
    apartment,
catch a train to the airport
and fly back to Canada ...
all in the same day.

There's no air conditioning,
the windows are sealed up tight,
it's 7:30 in the morning,
it's already twenty-eight degrees,
and we've been sitting on the bus waiting for it to leave for half
     an hour.

Ken seethes in frustration. He turns to Rita and snaps:

Ken: These people.
     They don't have the same ideas about being on time that
     we do.
     What?
     What did I say?

The bus pulls away from the station.

     7:33.
     About time.

     Don't worry.
     Last night I put a big bottle of water in the freezer.
     I can feel it against my side.
     Cool and soothing — a solid block of confidence against
          the interminable bus ride ahead.

     Yes, yes. This is the real thing, the way the real people travel.
     What is that woman doing ...?
     She's got a plastic bag to her face ...and she's...
     She's vomiting.
     I know, I know,
     just look at her black clothing, the traditional headscarf,
     I'm suffocating just looking at her.
     There she goes for another round.

     Oh, look, this woman is opening a window.
     Thank you.
     Finally, we'll get some air.
     Oh!
     Oh!

He turns around and looks behind; sees something even more shocking.

Oh!!
Oh!!!
We're surrounded by four puking women.
Hand me some water.

This is that frozen block of water we took out of the
    freezer two hours ago?
It's as warm as three-day-old camel milk.

Ken takes a sip and notices a small insect on the inside of his arm.

Whoa. Cockroach.
Hey Rita, there's one on your arm.

Ken flicks it to the ground. He tries to step on it and he sees ...

Ah!! There's hundreds of cockroaches on the floor.
Hundreds of cockroaches.
Ah!!!!!!!!
They're on the armrest,
on the seat,
there's one on your arm,
on my leg —
Oh no —
our olives! Our msemen.

Ken bends down to look at the bag of food.

We're going without lunch.

*Ken slowly pushes the bag of food to one side with his foot. He starts to
stomp on the bugs.*

And the cockroaches are only around our seat.
They are nowhere else on the bus.
We are the epicentre of the cockroach infestation.
It's like something out of a horror movie.
The ancient woman with no teeth who is sitting behind us.
is just laughing at the dirty Canadians who brought all
    the cockroaches on the bus.
"These are not my cockroaches!"

Rita, we're supposed to be Buddhists — are you sure this is right?

Hey we're not moving.

It's one o'clock, forty-three degrees and we're not going anywhere.
I dunno. There's an argument going on outside, in front of the bus.
The driver's trying to drive over the men who are blocking the bus —
he's trying to settle the argument by killing them.

Why is no one else on the bus unnerved about this at all?
Sometimes insha'llah is bad.

Argh!
We're hours away from getting home.
And we're stuck on a bus!

Ken clutches his chest.

I can't …
I can't …
I can't breathe —

Ken reaches out to one of the seats to steady himself, but he misses and slips to the floor, still clutching his chest. He crawls forward, desperately looking to the passengers for help, for anyone who can speak English.

I can't catch my —
This is what happened to Beth.

Ken faints and collapses to the floor. Everything is still for a moment. Ken becomes Burroughs. He stands, slips on the battered fedora, and looks down at where Ken was lying.

Burroughs: Look at you kid, holding your chest, not breathing.
You ought to listen to the girl, kiddo.
You can't change the world,
you can't get off the bus,
you're in it for the long haul.

Sure, your sister is dead, that's tough.
My sister died.
His sister died.
Her sister died.
That woman up there, her sister's going to die.
It happens.

It's like this:
When we are born, each of us is set adrift on an endless
    sea in a leaky canoe.
Sure, we can bail out the canoe as fast as we want, we can
    paddle as hard as we want,
we can lash our canoe to other canoes,
but sooner or later we all have to face the fact
that the boat is destined to sink.

Ken: No Mr. Burroughs, you don't understand.
    Just before we left
    I called Beth. I told her
    "Beth, I have proposed to Rita, I'm going to marry that
        woman and I don't care what you think."
    Beth said, "Okay … but I guess I'm not going to be asked
        to be a flower girl, huh?"
    I said, "Oh, come on Beth, you're only forty-one, it could
        happen."
    She was happy for me.
    She wanted to talk but I was still mad at her.
    I said I had to pack.
    I said I'd try to call her when I got back from Morocco.
    Mr. Burroughs we were supposed to make up
    and I missed my chance.

And with that I just …
right there, on the bus on the side of the road in Morocco on
    the northern tip of Africa…
I make the most fateful decision of my life.
I surrender.
I sit back in my seat and I let those cockroaches crawl all over
    me.

A few minutes later money changes hands,
the driver is back aboard and, miraculously, we're off.
Twenty minutes after that the bus stops for gas.
I go to the bathroom.
I poo.
There's a little toad in the corner.
It reminds me of Ibrahim's shop.

Rita buys more water.
It looks like a Molson's commercial
tiny beads of ice drip down the sides of the bottle
the crystal clear liquid is just one degree above freezing as it
    pours down my dusty throat.

Rita: Ken, are we going to be okay?

Ken: Yeah Rita, we are going to be just fine.

Rita: 'Cause I really love you.

Ken: I love you too Rita Bozi.

The bus pulls onto a coastal highway
Rita manages to force open a window
it's less than an hour before the bus pulls into Casablanca.
We're only three and half hours late.
In Morocco, that's like being on time!

Rita is spraying the ancient woman with no teeth who was sit-
    ting behind us
with an essential oil mist she keeps in her bag;
"Salaam Alaikum," the old woman says.

Peace be with you.
And all at once, in a wave, I realize I love this country, I love
    these people.
"Walaikum assalam," I say.
And peace also be upon you.

The woman clutches the bottle of essential oil mist to her breast
and she asks if she can keep it:
Rita is about to say yes

when she stops and thinks better of it and turns to me for my
    opinion.

Ken smiles. He shrugs.

Ken: Insha'llah.

* * *

We made it to Anthony's.
I took every article of clothing out of our bags and shook it
    out right there on the street.
Not a cockroach in sight.
Like it was all a figment of my imagination.
I took a shower, but I still felt like I had a fever.
I drank two litres of water and didn't even pee once.
It took a second shower and two vodkas to make me feel like
    I wasn't still on fire.
We had just enough time to repack before we had to head for
    the airport.
The flight to Canada was routine: *Starsky and Hutch* and
    maple-glazed Atlantic salmon.

My parents were in Ireland for a month,
but somehow I didn't mind as much as I thought I would.
We had a memorial service for Beth a few days after her forty-
    first birthday.
It was a beautiful, humid August day.
There was a discreet wooden box at the front that held her
    remains.
I never did get to see her body in the coffin, never did touch
    her face before she went into the cold, cold ground.

I did write a eulogy.
Everyone cried.
The family took the ashes to the graveyard.
As soon as we pulled up the drive it started to rain.
I thought to myself
"If this were a play it would have been the other way around —
    the sun would have come out."

But I try not to think about plays. Not all the time.

The funeral home guys gave everyone a black umbrella.

Mom and Dad had asked me to place the ashes in the ground,
and just before I did,

I stopped and looked back at the sea of black umbrellas

protecting all of our aunts and uncles and all of our cousins
and second cousins twice removed.

And I realized there was only one member of the family
missing.

And I felt a tear, just starting, right here.

When I returned home to Calgary I found a message from Beth
on my voicemail.

I'd totally forgotten I'd saved it.

It really shook me to hear that voice from beyond the grave.

But it felt good too.

It was like waking up from those dreams in Morocco —

for just an instant, I would think

"It's all just been a mistake,

Beth's just been hiding out in Vegas for a few months to teach
me a lesson."

Beth: *Voice-over.* Hey Ken, it's Beth.

I just called to see how exciting it was out there with
Calgary maybe bringing home the Stanley Cup ...

And just again the apology was absolutely heartfelt.

Nothing more I can do except that to say that I am truly
sorry

and I guess that's it.

I just thought ...

I am truly sorry.

Impersonal Machine Voice: End of message.

To erase this message press seven.

Sometimes, I think that my sister died because I broke her heart.

The way my voicemail works, once you archive a message,
the system asks if it can delete that message every forty-five days.

So far I have been saving that message for two years, nine months, and twenty days.

Ken tries to press seven. He can't.

Ken crosses upstage and turns around the last music stand. It is a picture of Beth.

Hi Beth.
Salaam Alaikum.

Pause.
The sound of the muezzin.
Ken walks offstage, leaving the picture behind.
Lights.

THE END

ENDNOTES

1 Despite how it is spelled, try saying it "sa-lam a-lay-koom." Every Muslim that you meet knows this expression, so it won't be hard to get pronunciation advice, although it might be a bit contradictory, depending upon regional dialect.

2 "Labes" seems to be specific to Darija, the Moroccan dialect, and most non-Moroccans are not familiar with it and will stare at you blankly. The other phrases, however, are universal across the Arabic world. Even non-Arab Muslims, who do not otherwise speak a word of Arabic, use some of these phrases.

3 Chefchaouen is pronounced in a variety of ways, none of them as it is spelled. I use "Shef-shah-wuan."

photo of April Banigan
as Marilyn Monroe
by Zoltan Varadi

MY ONE
AND ONLY

PLAYWRIGHT'S INTRODUCTION

My One And Only was the first play I wrote that I did not intend to direct.

Perhaps I should say it was the first play that I wrote *as a mature playwright* that I did not intend to direct. Early in my career, I had written some successful plays that got produced a few times, but the more they were produced the less happy I was with the results. The economics of theatre being what they were for a young emerging and largely untested playwright/director in Calgary in the mid-'90s, I ended up being a playwright/director/producer/publicist/grant-writer. And the more I wrote/directed/produced/publicized my own work, the more I found myself getting into a rut. Somehow the production I envisioned in my head was less and less like the productions I found onstage: less adventuresome, less exciting, less com-pelling, and yet conversely, more work.

At one point early in this process I happened across the novel *Civilization: And Its Part In My Downfall* by the gifted polymath Paul Quarrington. I had fallen in love with Kurt Vonnegut's *Slaughterhouse-Five* in high school and here I found a Canadian novelist working in a similar vein. I wrote to Quarrington and got his permission to adapt his novel, first as a screenplay in collaboration with a pair of friends, and later for the stage.

Civilization is a sprawling, non-linear epic about the early days of Hollywood westerns that mixes equal parts humour and pathos. In order to write the adaptation, we first had to analyze the work, and my comrades wrote each scene in the novel on a separate cue card, fairly common practice in screen-writing. Their ingenious twist was to colour-code each card to correspond with a plotline/timeline in the novel. When we had completed this Herculean task, we piled the hundred or so cards on the table in a neat stack, and found we could see

146 HARVEST and other plays by Ken Cameron

the ebb and flow of the various plotlines simply by following
the sequence of colours. What begins as a riot of colour at the
beginning of Paul's novel soon starts to sort itself out, with
particular plotlines gaining prominence as the novel unfolds:
first the green of the character's travels across country, then
the yellow of his days on the ranch, then the pale blue confusion of his life in Hollywoodland, all peppered with the pink
of his final days awaiting execution in prison.

Both manuscripts languish in a drawer to this day. But the
process was transformative for me as a playwright.

Years later, I happened across an article in *Saturday Night*
magazine about Marilyn Monroe shooting the film *River of
No Return* in Banff, complete with photos of her in a white
wool sweater against the backdrop of the Rockies and the
Banff Springs Hotel. The article spoke about how she injured
her leg on the shoot, and I wondered if perhaps it was this
accident that began the lifelong addiction to painkillers that
eventually killed her. The article recounted the story of three
boys who rode their bikes out from the set and happened
across Marilyn on the side of a gravel road, out for a walk.
Always a lover of children, Marilyn asked if she could borrow a bike. The author recalled how she squealed with girlish
delight as she wobbled down the road.

I put the article in a drawer.

As is so often the case with the best ideas, the seed that
was to become *My One And Only* needed time to germinate in
the fertile darkness of that drawer. My subconscious needed
time to equate what I had learned from Paul Quarrington
with what I had read in *Saturday Night*. But when it finally did,
I pulled out the leftover coloured cue cards I had used before
and began to jot down some random ideas. Then I began to
write a few scenes.

I began with the idea of a non-linear narrative and, like
Vonnegut, I used a science fiction metaphor as a structural
hook. What would happen, I wondered, if your first love were
Marilyn Monroe? Would any other woman ever measure up
in your mind? Would you ever escape your past? Or would you

always be trapped, endlessly circling back over the past, picking it apart over and over again. Like an atomic bomb that fractured the last century, such an event would forever divide your life into a "before" and an "after." I recalled the many times that my mind would wander back to events in my past that I regretted, and how visceral those memories seemed: one minute I was treating that girlfriend poorly, the next I was back washing dishes in my kitchen. I was eager to explore a character who was as unable to escape his past as I am.

The first two or three scenes started well enough: a policeman stopping a car on the side of the road; a secret; memories of a starlet in a small town; a mother who drinks. But then I started writing a scene with a big, epic, sweeping landscape. I pulled myself up short, halfway through, caught by the sudden realization that I had no idea how I would direct such a scene. My finger was poised over the delete button before I realized that the director part of my brain was already editing and limiting the playwright's creativity. And if I were doing that this early in the process, how could my playwriting possibly be served by directing my own work?

Still, it was some time before I was ready to give up directing this particular play. After the second draft, Alberta Theatre Projects asked if I would consider letting them stage it at their prestigious playRites Festival. I said no. I already had some grant money in hand, you see. Fortunately, my close friend and colleague Ron Jenkins — who had already committed to a one-week workshop at Edmonton's Workshop West Theatre — upbraided me with so much verbal abuse and good sense that I sheepishly returned to ATP the following week asking if they still had a slot left.

It was this decision to allow other directors to collaborate on my work that allowed me to grow and mature as a playwright. By resisting the urge to direct, I was able to focus more of my attention on the job of playwriting; by relinquishing control over the means of production, I was able to let others do what they do well and allow myself to focus on following my passion.

I do not regret "the ten lost years" I spent directing my own plays. I provided myself with the best self-education in independent theatre possible, learning intimately the challenges faced by members of the production team. But I owe a great debt of thanks to my collaborators Ron, Vanessa, Bob, and Gail, who turned my attention back to my one true love — writing plays.

ACKNOWLEDGMENTS

These thanks must be reproduced in the program of any production of the play:

My One and Only premiered at the Enbridge playRites Festival of New Canadian Plays in 2004, produced by Alberta Theatre Projects.

My One and Only was developed with the assistance of Alberta Playwrights' Network (which receives funding support from Theatre Alberta), Workshop West Theatre and the Springboards New Play Festival, and the 2002 and 2003 Banff Playwrights Colony (which is a partnership between the Canada Council for the Arts, the Banff Centre for the Arts, and Alberta Theatre Projects).

Ken Cameron is a member of the Playwrights Guild of Canada.

Special thanks to: Ron Jenkins, Bob White, Vanessa Porteous, Eddie Hunter, Dave Lange, Allister & Carolyn Cameron, and Rita Bozi.

PERFORMANCES

My One and Only premiered at the Enbridge playRites Festival of New Canadian Plays in 2004, produced by Alberta Theatre Projects with the following cast:

Marilyn/Lilly: Tara Hughes
Policeman/Rev. Clark/Townie: Trevor Leigh
Mom: Heather Lea MacCallum
Scout: Kevin MacDonald

PRODUCTION
Director: Gail Hanrahan
Set Designer: Scott Reid
Lighting Designer: Jeff Logue
Costume Designer: Jenifer Darbellay
Composer and Sound Designer: Kevin McGugan
Fight Director: J-P Fournier
Production Dramaturg: Vanessa Porteous
Production Stage Manager: Dianne Goodman
Stage Manager: Rhonda Kambeitz

It was subsequently produced by Workshop West in Edmonton in April 2005, with the following cast:

Marilyn/Lilly: April Banigan
Policeman/Rev. Clark/Townie: Glenn Nelson
Mom: Annette Loiselle
Scout: Chris Fassbender

PRODUCTION
Director: Ron Jenkins
Production Designer: Narda McCarroll
Sound Designer: Chris Wynters
Stage Manager: Cheryl Millikin
Production Manager: Scott Peters

STAGING

The play is set in both 1953 and 1962 in both Banff and Los Angeles.

Several locations are required, including a hotel room, a car, a movie theatre, the porch of a house and a mountainside. Rather than being literal, a design should be poetic, allowing for easy and instantaneous transition from one location to another. Many of these transitions might be best accomplished through the use of light, sound, or imagination.

A NOTE ON STAGING

My One and Only is a fictional account of the time Marilyn Monroe spent in Banff and Jasper shooting the film *River of No Return* in 1953. I have taken great liberties with the facts surrounding the shooting of the film. While it is true that Marilyn shot the film in Canada, in both Banff and Jasper National Parks, everything else in the play is pure fiction. Audiences and readers alike should be warned that the facts tend to get in the way and diminish one's enjoyment of the story.

Marilyn Monroe is a modern icon — as powerful and pervasive to us as images of the goddess were to cultures in ages past. Even those who take little interest in her life cannot escape her extensive influence. This play is not by any means a biography of Marilyn Monroe, even though a Marilyn impersonation is critical to its telling. While she figures largely in the story, the Marilyn of this play is her own creature, as much a fictional creation as the other characters. The figure of Marilyn and the details of her visit to Canada are the starting point, not the facts of the case.

It is partly the story of our culture's fascination with Marilyn Monroe, and partly a variation on that stalwart of Canadian literature — the coming-of-age story. Ultimately, it is a play about the trials of becoming a man.

It is my belief that a script is only a blueprint for production, and that it is an error to mistake the text for the play. Directors and actors are therefore invited to give free rein to their imaginations and to discover inventive ways to stage the episodic scenes.

Dialogue and some songs from the film *River of No Return* have *not* been quoted in the text. While the script may suggest the inclusion of images in one form or another, these choices are left to the director's discretion. Directors may feel free to make as much — or as little — use of the film in other ways as they see fit, but are warned that the film is under copyright.

"Those who genuinely loved her never fell
out of love with her — in spite of everything."
Neil Sinyard, biographer

"The past didn't go anywhere."
Utah Phillips, storyteller

MY ONE AND ONLY
The Movies

Scout is watching a movie. The light plays across his face, flickering. The sound of an old-fashioned projector and muffled dialogue from a film can be heard indistinctly. Scout begins to sing softly along with the film.

An old battered pocket watch dangles from Scout's hand.

Scout: It's 1945 and a watch is stopping. It's 1953 and she's on my bike. It's 1945 and a bomb is dropping. It's 1962 and I'm speeding down the highway.

A man enters shining his flashlight; he might look like an usher, or a night watchman.

One minute I'm fifteen, the two of us, warm skin in the Cave and Basin. And the next, it's 1962 and I'm stopped for speeding outside of Los Angeles.

A tear stains Scout's cheek. He holds his head in his hands. The man shines the light in Scout's face.

Man: Well, this is a depressing start.

Los Angeles, 1962

*Scout has been stopped at the side of the road. The Man, a **Policeman**, shines the light in his eyes.*

Policeman: I said, "Well, this is a depressing start."

Scout sits up. He stares straight ahead, stone-faced, saying nothing. Silence.

That's supposed to be a joke. *Silence.* A conversation starter. *Silence.* An ice-breaker. *Silence.* Speaking of ice-breakers, I see you're from Canada. Got that off the plates. *Silence.* Any idea how fast you were goin', son?

Scout: Uh … not really.

Policeman: A hunret. Miles. An hour. Know what the speed limit is?

Scout: Um … Fifty-five?

Policeman: It's a residential street.

Scout: Thirty-five?

Policeman: And a school zone.

Scout shakes his head, nervous.

You know, when my granddad was a kid, they built the first train that could go near a hunret miles an hour. Doctors were afraid that people would get hurt from going so fast. They thought people's brains would get squashed against the back of the cranial cavity from the excessive speed. *Pause.* The speed limit in a school zone is twenty-five miles an hour. That puts you how far over the speed limit?

Scout: I'm not sure.

Policeman: A hunret minus twenty-five is …?

Scout: Seventy-five.

Policeman: Seventy-five miles an hour over the speed limit. Enough to squash your brain. Can I see your license, son?

Scout hands over his license. The Policeman looks at it angrily.

You are aware this ain't a laughin' matter?

Scout: Yes sir.

Policeman: A hunret miles an hour, that's a serious violation of the California Highway Safety Code. You do know that, don't you?

Scout: Yes sir.

Policeman: So, keeping yer serious violation of the California Highway Safety Code in the forefront of yer mind, you wouldn't be pullin' my prick, would ya … *Checks the name on the license.* Would ya, Scout?

Scout: I would not be pulling your prick, sir.

Policeman: *Holding up the driver's license.* Banf…f…f?

Scout: It's where I live. It's a real town.

Policeman: Huh. What brings you to Hollywood in such a rush, Scout?

Scout leans forward in his chair, holding his head in his hands, as before.

Coming to Town

Scout stands. He is holding a copy of Life *magazine, with Marilyn Monroe on the cover.* **Mom** *has a glass of whiskey in her hand.*

Mom: What are you doing?

Scout: Nothing.

Mom: What are you doing with my magazine?

Scout: Just looking.

Mom: At pictures of girls? *Snatches the magazine.* Of that Marilyn Monroe? Huh?

Scout: Yeah. She's pretty. She reminds me of you.

Mom: Me?

Mom looks at the picture.

Scout: Kind of.

Mom: Well. That's a nice thing to say to your old Mom.

Scout: You're not old.

She tousles his hair. He instinctively smoothes it.

Mom: What would you say if your old Mom told you she'd take you to see Marilyn Monroe?

Scout: Are we going to the movies?

Mom: Better than that. How'd you like to see Marilyn Monroe in person?

Scout: Golly! Are we going to Hollywood?

Mom: We don't have to. Hollywood is coming to us. Right here, in Banff. Reverend Clark says they're making a movie here next month.

Scout: Here in town? Wow!

Mom: And if you're a good boy, maybe your old Mom will take you to the station when the train comes in. Maybe if you take a bath and dress up real nice, your old Mom will introduce you to the stars, Robert Mitchum and Marilyn Monroe.

Scout: Marilyn Monroe? She's so pretty.

Mom: But you have to be good.

Scout: I'll be good, I promise!

Mom: Now leave Mommy alone for a bit.

Mom pours herself another drink from the whiskey bottle under her chair.

Scout: OK. Geez. Marilyn Monroe.

Mud Puddles

Scout and the Policeman.

Policeman: Do you want to step out of the car, please, son?

Scout: Is there anything wrong, Officer?

Policeman: Just step out of the car, son.

Scout: It's a real town. I know the name sounds a little funny.

Policeman: Out of the car.

Scout steps out of the car. The Policeman shines the flashlight on his legs. They are muddy.

> Been playing in the mud puddles?

Scout: I was taking a walk in the park. I strayed off the path. Couldn't find my way back. I followed a creek. Slipped on the bank and fell in.

Policeman: Funny it's just your legs.

Scout: I rinsed my hands off in the water.

Policeman: Which park?

Scout: I don't remember.

Policeman: There's not a lot of parks around here, Scout. We got cities in America. Pavement. Steel girders. Glass. Maybe the odd tree. Not many parks.

Scout: Guess I found the only one.

Policeman: We got a lot of big estates in America. Could be mistaken for a park — if you was an idiot. But they're private property. You sure you weren't trespassing?

Scout: It was a park.

Policeman: You climb over a fence to get to that park, Scout?

Scout: No.

Policeman: Maybe squeeze through a gate?

Scout: It was a park.

Policeman: You didn't see any dogs, did ya? Sometimes these parks, the private ones, they're guarded by dogs. Vicious things. They'll chase you. Known folks to fall down when they're chased by dogs. Sometimes they get muddy. Like you.

Scout: I went for a walk. In a public park. I didn't see any signs that said it was private.

Policeman: You wouldn't mind if I took a look in your car, would ya?

Scout: I'd rather you didn't.

Policeman: Why's that? Ain't got nuthin' to hide, do ya?

Scout: Look, unless you have probable cause —

Policeman: Why don't you just stand over there. Just over there.

Scout sighs and steps aside. The Policeman sits down inside the car and begins to poke around.

Lots of folk I stop, they think they can get away with saying nothing. Never works. Sooner or later, everyone feels the need to speak. It's a primal urge. Goes back to the campfire. Flames flickering. Rough stone walls. Shadows. Talking keeps the evil spirits at bay. Did you know that?

The Policeman shines the light on Scout's face. He shifts his feet uncomfortably.

I'll just bet you got a few evil spirits, don't you Scout?

Spin the Bottle

Mom knocks over the bottle. It rolls to a stop at Scout's feet. He picks it up.

Scout: It's 1953 and I'm fifteen, right before she became My One and Only. The tourists go to the big Cave and Basin, but we kids, we got another place, the *secret* Cave and Basin, up the hill a ways. It's fed by the same hot springs, but it's condemned, so no one comes here. The girls want it that way. They ain't gonna do nothing, they say, unless it's in the secret Cave and Basin, one at a time.

Scout spins the bottle on the ground. It comes to a rest before he continues.

We used the bottle to pick partners. I got Lilly Clark, the preacher's daughter.

Lilly appears in a spot. They are in a cave, damp and dripping, womb-like; their voices echo strangely.

Scout: So?

Lilly: So?

Scout: So take your top off.

Lilly: No.

Scout: You have to. We're partners.

Lilly: So? Doesn't mean I have to show you my boobs.

Scout: You show me all the time.

Lilly: No I don't.

Scout: Do too.

Lilly: I show Bobby. You're eavesdropping.

Scout: You can't eavesdrop with your eyes.

Lilly: You're sneaking a peek.

Scout gets a nickel from his pocket.

Scout: Give you a nickel.

Lilly: I'm not going to show you my boobs for a nickel.

Scout: The Mercer twins show Bobby their boobs. Four for a nickel. Besides, you have to. There's a competition.

Lilly: What competition?

Scout: To see who makes the earth move.

Lilly: What are you talkin' about?

Scout: If the girl's reaction is big, then the guy who's doing it, he's made the earth move. Because the girl is hollerin'.

Lilly: What do you mean hollerin'?

Scout: You know. Hollerin'. "Oh baby." "Hello Daddy." All that.

Lilly: Is that what they do?

Scout: Yeah.

Lilly: Bobby doesn't.

Scout: Does so. With Jenny Mercer. He says she's a real hollerer.

Lilly: You're makin' it up.

Scout: I ain't.

Scout reaches into his pocket.

I'll give you two.

Lilly: Ten cents!?

Scout: It's all I got. My Mom doesn't give me an allowance.

Lilly sighs and flashes her boobs, real quick.

That's not enough.

Lilly: That's all you get.

Scout: You gotta make the noise.

Lilly: No.

Scout: You have to. Or it doesn't count.

Lilly: Oh baby.

Scout: They gotta be able to hear it.

Lilly: Oh baby!

She reaches for the nickels. Scout holds them back.

Scout: Now the other one.

Lilly: Hello Daddy! There. Happy?

She reaches for the nickels. Scout holds them back.

Scout: Show me your boobs again.

Lilly: You can't buy my boobs. They aren't real estate.

Scout: I just want to look.

Lilly: Just 'cause your Mom's a whore doesn't mean every girl on earth is.

Silence. Scout turns this thought over in his mind, fuming.

Scout: *To himself.* Mom's not a whore.

Lilly: I don't need your stupid ten cents.

Scout: My Mom's not a whore.

Lilly: Like the whore of Babylon. That's what my Dad says.

Lilly starts to walk away.

Scout: Your Dad comes to my house.

Lilly comes back slowly, uncertain.

Lilly: Does not.

Scout: Tuesday nights, at the end of the month. After he visits the shut-ins.

Lilly: My Dad's a preacher.

Scout: Why do you think it takes him five hours to visit four old ladies? An hour each, and then an hour at my house. I'm supposed to be asleep, but sometimes I peek through the hole where the stovepipe used to be.

Lilly: You're a liar.

Scout: Your Dad has a birthmark on his bum. Looks like a … a … mushroom cloud.

Lilly crosses her arms, covering her breasts.

   Shouting. "That's it! Oh baby! Hallelujah!" That's what your Dad says the last Tuesday night of the month.

He tosses the nickels at her feet.

   I've seen your tits.

Dirty Little Boys

Scout stands, guiltily. Mom is as shocked as she is furious.

Mom: Lilly Clark? The preacher's daughter? You asked the preacher's daughter ... to show you her ... dirties?

Scout: She started it.

Mom: Lilly Clark is a nice girl. I've served tea with her in the church basement.

Scout: She did.

Mom: Girls don't start things like that. Girls don't have dirty minds.

Scout: Lilly Clark does. She's —

Mom smacks him.

Mom: Girls don't have dirty minds. Boys do. Dirty little boys who can't keep their filthy minds off their nasty little bits and who lead nice girls astray. I won't have Lilly Clark led astray, not by a boy of mine.

Scout: I wasn't.

Mom: Did you stick it in her?

Scout: Mom!

Mom: Did you stick your thing in her?

Scout: No!

Mom: Good.

Pause. Mom is frightened by her own reaction. She tries to be more reasonable, but only succeeds in appearing unpredictable.

You don't know what you're getting into, Scout. It's dangerous territory down there. It's led more than one person in this family astray. *Pause.* You have your father's nose, did I ever tell you that?

Scout: Yes.

Mom: And his eyes. You have his eyes.

Scout: I have your eyes. You always said.

Mom: Not if you want to be looking at Lilly Clark's bits, they're
not. They're his eyes now. Oh, Scout. It seems like fun
now. Makes you tingle all over. Makes you feel all grown
up. But you're not a grown-up. And if you start acting like
one, who do you think is going to have to clean up the
mess, huh?

Scout: We was just foolin', Mom.

Mom: Do you want to take care of a baby? Huh? Do you?
Because that's what happens when you start fooling
around with little girls' bits. It's like an atom bomb, that
thing there, and when it goes off … If you make a baby,
there's no way I'm letting you keep it, not like I did,
I should have —

Mom stops short. She's horrified at what she's said.

Scout: We didn't mean anything.

Mom: We never do, sweetie. We never do.

Silence. Mom seems exhausted, spent.

I don't want you thinking any more about your little
fellow … Not until you're married. You keep your atom
bomb in your pants until after you have said your vows
in a church of God.

The doorbell rings.

You are not allowed to touch it. And no one else is either.

Scout: What if I have to pee?

Mom: *Almost tenderly.* Don't you talk back to me. You know
what I mean. Now go to your room.

Scout: Mom …

The doorbell rings again.

Mom: Go to your room. You're being punished. That's Reverend Clark, I'm sure. I'm going to have to make it up to him.

Mom opens the door. **Reverend Clark** *stands in the door. He is gravely concerned.*

Rev. Clark: Where is he?

Mom: Awful sorry about all this, Ernie.

Rev. Clark: How many times do I have to come over to talk to that boy of yours, Flo?

Mom: Yes, I know —

Rev. Clark: And now this? My own daughter?

Mom: I've already spoken to him.

Rev. Clark marches over to Scout.

Rev. Clark: What did you say to her?

Mom: Ernie, stop —

Rev. Clark: What did you tell her?

Mom: Ernie! *To Scout.* Go to your room, I said. *To Rev. Clark.* You're just making it worse, Ernie.

Scout: I wasn't —

Mom: You're not leavin' this house until you learn to stay away from that filthy cave. And from now on you can leave the door open when you pee.

Scout: Does this mean I can't go see Marilyn Monroe?

Mom: No you can not. You can go to school and you can come right home again, Marilyn Monroe or no Marilyn Monroe. Now go to your room.

Scout starts off.

Rev. Clark: Just a minute. Scout ... You are at an age, when a boy's body is changing ... those changes can sometimes influence a boy's imagination with ... impure thoughts ... I don't know what you *think* you may have seen on Tuesday nights. But I'm a family man, son. A family man.

Scout: Yes sir.

Rev. Clark: There's a good lad.

Mom: Go to your room.

Scout crosses to a separate spot, his room. After a moment he can hear Mom and Rev. Clark downstairs.

Rev. Clark: It's not going to be any easier for you if word of this gets out.

Mom: Now Ernie ... sweetie ... It's not going to get out. We can keep this ... thing ... just between us ... Can't we, sweetie?

Scout: If I close my eyes ...

Mom: Nobody else needs to know, do they, Ernie ...?

Scout: If I close my eyes and remember the future ...

Mom: You know I can make it worth your while.

Scout: ... if I remember Marilyn ...

Mom: It won't happen again. I'll take care of him.

Scout: ... then none of this matters ...

Mom: I'll take care of him.

The mournful sound of a train whistle is heard in the distance.

Scout: ... none of this matters ...

The train arrives. Scout opens his eyes. He stands on his tiptoes.

The whole town crowds the platform, the day she comes to town. 'Cept me. I'm in my room.

Distant applause. Scout strains to see.

> Stupid Lilly Clark and her stupid boobs. Now I'll never get to see Marilyn.

He comes down off his tiptoes. He's missed it all.

Nice Bike

Marilyn appears in a spot, wearing a scarf over her hair and dark sunglasses. Scout is holding a bicycle. In the basket on the front of the bike is a paper bag of groceries and a bottle of whiskey. Marilyn looks at him. Scout stares back open-mouthed.

Marilyn: Nice bike.

Scout: Thanks.

Marilyn: Is that a ... Raleigh?

Scout: No.

Marilyn: What is it then?

Scout: A hand-me-down.

Marilyn: Can I go for a ride?

Scout: Aren't you Marilyn Monroe?

Marilyn: Shh. Don't tell anyone. I'm incognito.

Scout: Everyone in town knows who you are.

Marilyn: Oh.

Marilyn starts to remove her glasses, then thinks better of it.

> Still. You gonna give me a ride?

Scout: Sure.

Marilyn climbs on the bike. She is unsteady.

> You want me to hold you?

Marilyn: My … aren't you the gentleman.

Scout blushes. He holds the bike for her. She squeals with delight.

Phone Ringing (1)

A phone rings in the blackout. Several times.

Scout: Hello?

Homes of the Hollywood Stars

Scout stands off to the side. The Policeman is going through the front seat of the car.

Policeman: When I say California, you think Hollywood. Don't you? Well, I live in Los Angeles.

The Policeman pulls a map from the front seat.

> That's why you won't find my house on one of these here maps to the "Homes of the Hollywood Stars." Me, I live way over here, about three feet off the side of the map. Found this in your glove box. Do you mind? *Stares at the map.* James Cagney's house. Did you see that one? Big pink house? Who'd of thought James Cagney would live in a pink house? Huh? Next to it is William Holden's. It's white. And down here, around the corner, is Rock Hudson's house.

He leans in closely, conspiratorially.

> Hudson's a fudge-packer. His house is blue. You'd think he'd have the pink one. Is that what you were doin' with the map? Lookin' to pack fudge with Hollywood royalty? You know every single person that's ever become a star has had to pack fudge to get there? Especially the girls. Marilyn Monroe — she took all of the Warner brothers at the same time … all four of 'em up the poop chute.

Scout: She did not.

Policeman: You got to do it. The only way to the top is through the bottom.

Scout: You take that back.

The policeman puts his hand on his gun.

Policeman: Or you'll what?

Scout forces himself to relax. After a beat, the Policeman relaxes also and looks at the map again.

> Oh. Lookee. You got Miss Monroe's house circled on this here map. That's a coincidence, ain't it?

Scout: Why's that?

Policeman: We was just talking about how she got ahead in the movie business. That's what got you all riled up.

Scout: I guess it was.

Policeman: You got any … special feelings for Miss Monroe?

Scout: She's a star.

Policeman: Sure is. Lots of people, they like stars. Do you like stars?

Scout: Who doesn't?

Policeman: Me for one. In this town, stars get away with murder. I stopped a speeder last week — I won't mention any names seein' as how that seems to upset you so much — but I pull this fella over because he is receiving oral sex while driving. Didn't seem to see how getting sucked off while operating a moving vehicle was a violation of the California Highway Safety Code. Next day, the sergeant comes up to me with the ticket in his hand and tears it up. Right in front of all the other guys. Seems some folk, just 'cause they're stars they can do no wrong. *Pause.* What was I just saying?

Scout: I don't remember.

Policeman: Stars... Starlets... Houses... That's right. You got Marilyn Monroe's house circled on this map.

Scout: It's just a map.

Policeman: Did you come down here for the big Marilyn Monroe funeral on Sunday?

Scout: Not exactly.

Policeman: Ever since she died, a lot of people they been coming down here just to gawk at her house. You been there?

Scout: Nope.

Policeman: Didn't go for a walk on her property?

Scout: Nope.

Policeman: Didn't climb over the fence thinking it was a park?

Scout: Nope.

The Policeman holds out the map to Scout.

Policeman: You see, the thing is, it's the only house you got circled. You ain't even got James Cagney's house circled. Out of all the places on this map, it's Marilyn Monroe's house what's marked out special. And yet you tell me you ain't even been there.

Scout: Thought I'd go tomorrow, when the weather's better.

Policeman: The thing is ... Marilyn Monroe's house was broken into tonight.

Scout: Really?

Policeman: Seems someone stole one of them costumes she kept from all those movies.

Scout: People these days.

Policeman: It's kind of sad, really. These people who feel

compelled to collect bits of their favourite stars. As if some clothing they've worn is the same thing as the star herself. Normally they steal something kinky — like underwear. That's what's so strange about this case, don't you think?

Scout: I don't know what you mean.

Policeman: They didn't steal anything kinky. Just an old pair of red shoes.

Everyone Knew Her

Scout sits in a chair. The flickering light plays on his face.

Scout: When the movie came out, the studio donated this special CinemaScope print to the library — as a memento for the whole town. But nobody's got a projector. Except me. I got it from the old Capital Theatre in Silverton for a song. Then I signed the film out from the library. It's years overdue. Every Saturday night I plug the projector into the wall, thread the film into the machine, hang the sheet from the ceiling. It's just you and me tonight, Marilyn.

The film plays on the screen.

Here in Banff everyone feels as if they knew her. Everyone claims they shook her hand, or talked to her, or were her friend. But it's a lie. She had no friends.

Defective Bike

Marilyn lies on the floor, the bicycle upturned beside her. The groceries are scattered across the ground. The bottle of whiskey is broken. Scout kneels, holding her ankle.

Marilyn: Ooooow!

Scout: Sorry.

Marilyn: You gave me a defective bike.

Scout: It's not defective.

Marilyn: Is so. And it broke my ankle.

Scout: It's just a sprain. Put some ice on it. It'll be fine in a few days.

Marilyn: A few days! They're going to kill me. I'm not supposed to do anything risky. Why did you let go of the bike?

Scout: I thought you'd know how to ride a bike.

Marilyn: I never had parents to teach me.

Scout: Oh.

Scout starts gathering the groceries.

Marilyn: Say ... are you an orphan? I can spot an orphan right away. It's a ... gift.

He picks up the broken bottle of whiskey and stares at it.

Scout: I've got a Mom.

Marilyn: Is that who the whiskey's for?

Scout nods.

   I'll pay for it.

Scout: It's OK. I can get another. She's on credit.

Marilyn: I've got a mother too. But I'm still an orphan.

Scout: You can't be an orphan if you have a Mom.

Marilyn: You can so. Believe me. My mother never kissed me. Not once. Never held me close, or gave me a hug. Not even a pat on the back. Even when she was OK. And then, one time — it was the middle of the night and I woke up from a deep, deep sleep — and there was my mother with her hands around my neck. She was going to strangle me. I just know it. She was in and out of institutions for years after that. So was I, orphanages or foster homes. I'm that kind of an orphan.

Scout: I guess I'm that kind of orphan too. Sort of.

Marilyn: *Smiling.* I knew it.

Model T

The Policeman walks around the car suspiciously. Scout watches nervously.

Policeman: This is a nice car. You like it?

Scout: It's OK.

Policeman: Better than when I was your age. The first car I ever had? A Model T Ford. Remember those? Model T? Probably not. It was my Dad's before he gave it to me. Your Dad give you this car?

Scout does not answer.

This your Dad's car?

Scout: No.

Pause.

Policeman: So. Whaddaya think?

Scout: About the Model T?

Policeman: About someone goes to all that trouble to break into a house full of stuff and all they take is a pair of red shoes? You think that's all they stole?

Scout: I wouldn't know.

Policeman: No? *Pause.* Whaddaya figure is so special about a pair of red shoes? *Pause.* The thing about the Model T was, it didn't have a trunk. The whole family'd go for a drive on Sundays, to the beach, but we'd have to keep all the picnic stuff on our laps — blanket, basket, bottle of ginger beer. Knowing there was a fresh-baked peach pie right there on my lap ... When I was a kid, I used to look at all the other cars on the road and I used to think, "Why can't we have a trunk?"

The Policeman stops at the rear of the car. He looks at Scout.

You want to open the trunk, Scout?

Keep Your Old Mom Company

Night. Mom is sitting in a chair. Her whiskey bottle is empty. She is half asleep. Scout enters with a fresh bottle. He tries to sneak past without waking her. Mom opens her eyes.

Mom: Did you bring it? You said you'd bring it by six.

Scout: I got held up.

Scout gives her the bottle.

Mom: Where you been?

Scout: Out.

Mom: Out where?

Scout: Just out.

Mom: C'mere. *Pause.* C'mere.

Scout steps towards her. Mom fondles his damp hair, gently. Scout tries to pull away. Mom tightens her grip on his hair.

You were out in that cave. Weren't you? Weren't you?

Scout wrenches himself free.

You know you're not supposed to go there. Don't you? Don't you know that?

Scout: Yeah.

Mom: Then why'd you do it for? Were you with a girl?

Long silence.

Mom: Get your cup.

Scout: Mom …

Mom: Get it.

Scout gets an old tin cup. Mom beckons him towards her. Scout sits beside her. Mom pours a splash of whiskey into his cup.

Keep your old Mom company fer a while.

They sit in silence. Mom drinks from her cup. Scout doesn't touch his.

Your father used to drink with me, on nights like this. Quiet and cool summer nights. Back when you were just a little baby crying in your crib.

Mom tousles Scout's hair. She draws his head into her lap and continues stroking his hair gently.

He made me leave you in your room. Your father said it wasn't right for babies to be around liquor. I don't know why, since he told me to rub it on your gums to stop you from cryin' when you were teething. But he wouldn't have you in the same room as an open bottle. So you'd cry yourself to sleep. I guess it doesn't matter much — you being around liquor — since you're not a little baby anymore.

Silence. Mom begins to sing a lullaby.

Scout: Mom was always waiting for my Dad. She never admitted it, but I know that's what she was doing, secretly, when she sat on the porch, drinking her whiskey, staring down the road. The house was falling apart, but she refused to even consider moving.

Mom: What's the difference?

Scout: He'd never know where to find her. It didn't make any sense to me for years, but I figured it out eventually. This is where she lived when he left —

Mom: *Bitterly.* What's the difference?

Scout: So it was where she hoped — expected — he would return.

Silence. Scout is warm, contented and safe in her bosom.

Why did Dad leave?

Mom: He just did. The earth moved that night, the night he left.

Scout: What's that mean, the earth moved?

Mom: Nothing.

Scout: Does it mean you loved him?

Mom emerges from her reverie and sets her mouth. She forces Scout from her lap.

Mom: No. Must have been some geological thing. They dropped the bomb on Japan right about then. Maybe it was that.

Scout: Do you remember, Dad gave me this watch to hold onto that night? It broke. Maybe that was the atom bomb too, 'cause ever since, it's run wonky — sometimes it skips forwards, sometimes back.

Mom: Drink up. It's time you got to bed. Mommy's got company coming.

Scout sniffs his cup and grimaces. But he takes a sip anyway. Rev. Clark enters. He is backlit so that we can't see his face. Mom sits up hopefully.

Scout: It happened most nights around 9:15. Someone would come off the main road, down our little street, lit from behind by the streetlights. You couldn't see their face at first, just this man coming up to the house. Maybe … maybe …

Rev. Clark: Isn't it a bit late for a lad his age to be up?

Mom sits back in her chair.

Mom: Time for bed, Scout.

Scout: It bugged me that Mom was always waiting for my Dad.

Mom: Go on.

Scout: I realized, long before Mom ever did, that he was
never going to come home, and there wasn't any point
in being lonely.

Mom: *Tired, uninterested.* How much you got, Ernie? Enough
for a shut-in?

Rev. Clark laughs coarsely.

Scout: It would bug me that these men, the preachers and
doctors that called her names around their own dinner
tables in front of their own children, names that would
make their way to my ears in the schoolyards and caves,
would take advantage of her loneliness.

Rev. Clark hands Mom a few bills.

Mom: Yeah. That'll do.

Scout: They were just there to fill the time, while she waited
for her One and Only. For the one that made the earth
move. One thing I've noticed, living my life in atomic
time — sometimes forward, sometimes back — is that waiting for the past to come back to you ain't all it's cracked
up to be. But then ... every once in a while ...

On the Side of Rocky Mountain (1)

*Marilyn lies on the ground, her head up on one arm. Scout is shovel-
ing. Scout flips some dirt her way. She laughs. They smile together.*

Marilyn: Leave that.

Scout: Can't. They want it done before first light tomorrow.
How's your ankle?

Marilyn: Better. I'm still taking those pills though.

Scout: Sorry about that.

Marilyn: You'll just have to make it up to me.

She smiles. Scout blushes. She stares up at the mountain.

> Our mountain. It's got a ... special place in my heart.
> Like it knows who I am. Like it's been waiting its whole
> life for me to come here and make my movie. It'd be a
> shame to leave it, and never see it again. Someday, I want
> to be buried here. On the side of Rocky Mountain.

Pause.

Scout: Am I ... your One and Only?

Marilyn: Oh Scout ... you're so young.

Scout: Never mind that. Am I?

She sighs. A whistle offstage. Marilyn sits up.

Marilyn: That'll be the crew. They must be ready for me.

*She stands. She reaches over and gives him a peck on the cheek. She
exits. Scout stares after her. He starts to sing the movie music to himself.
Scout throws up his arms dramatically, standing on the edge of the
mountain. Perhaps the rest of the cast joins him from the shadows.*

How Old Are You?

Scout in a spot. Marilyn in another spot.

Scout: *River of No Return.* That was the movie Marilyn shot
in Banff that summer we met.

The spots merge. Scout stares at Marilyn, transfixed.

Marilyn: I play Kay, the most beautiful woman in the whole
wild west, but also, the loneliest. I'm married to Rory
Calhoun, a gambler who wins a claim in a card game.
When there are no horses and the river proves to be

impassable, Rory does the unthinkable ... He deserts
Kay — the most beautiful woman in the whole wild west,
but also, the loneliest. She flees down the river, taking
Robert Mitchum and his young son with her ... Scout,
are you listening?

Scout: How old are you?

Marilyn: How do you expect to be able to help me with my
lines if you don't know the plot of the film?

Scout: I dunno. How old are you?

Marilyn: What kind of question is that?

Scout: In the movies you're all grown up. But in person, you
don't seem grown up. It's like you're two ages at the same
time. It's weird.

Marilyn: Celluloid bleaches the skin and the transformative
power of the lens magnifies even the tiniest features of
the human face. This is a fact. Jack Palance isn't really
ugly. The Three Stooges are quite ordinary-looking.
Jean Harlow didn't even have a good side. I was married
by the time I was your age, Scout. My Aunt Grace — she
wasn't really my aunt, just a friend of my mother's who
took me in. But I thought of her as my aunt — for a while
at least. Until she told me I either had to marry the boy
next door or go back to the orphanage. And I wasn't
going back there for love nor money. Boy, was I a sight!
An ugly little duckling with a big nose and small boobs,
marrying a boy I'd barely even spoken to —

Scout: You don't have small boobs. Lilly Clark, she has really
small boobs —

Scout stops speaking, blushing.

Marilyn: Have you seen Lilly Clark's boobs?

Scout: No.

Marilyn: Yes you have.

Scout: She showed Bobby. I eavesdropped.

Marilyn: You can't eavesdrop with your eyes.

Scout: I snuck a peek.

Marilyn: And Lilly Clark has small boobs?

Scout: They're OK.

Marilyn: Are they bigger than mine?

Scout: I haven't seen yours.

Marilyn: Well … maybe you will someday. *Silence.* Why don't you be my adopted son?

Scout: *Startled.* What?

Marilyn tosses him the script. She produces a pair of red shoes from her bag.

Marilyn: Kay has just been rescued from the raging river. She's polishing her shoes.

Scout: Uh … OK.

Marilyn: Everything she owns has just been swept downstream. All that she has left to her name are her guitar and her treasured pair of red shoes.

Marilyn breathes a few times, to prepare herself. With a deep breath she assumes the position: she begins polishing a pair of shoes. They run a few lines. Marilyn doesn't like the way the last line of their dialogue sounds. She repeats it, trying to get it right. Scout stares transfixed as the lights fade.

When Did You Lose Your Mother?

Mom is sitting in her chair, her bottle at her feet. She is barely conscious, but she manages to lock eyes with Scout. He looks at her for a moment as Marilyn continues to run her one line over and over again, like a film stuck in a gate.

Mementoes

Scout and the Policeman. The Policeman holds out his hand.

Policeman: What about it, Scout? Got the keys?

Scout gives him the keys. The Policeman starts off towards the rear of the car.

Scout: Sometimes you want a memento.

The Policeman stops.

> Something to remember a person by. That's what those handprints in the cement are all about. The ones at the Walk of Fame — outside that theatre — what's it called …

Policeman: Grauman's Chinese Theatre.

Scout: Right. You can put your hand in the cement and pretend you're holding hands with Rita Hayworth.

Policeman: Or Marilyn Monroe?

The Policeman starts off towards the rear of the car again.

Scout: OK, you got me.

The Policeman stops.

> I wanted to find a memento. Some part of her that I could hang onto. When I was a kid, they had that saying carved into the — what do you call it? — the altar in the church. "This do in remembrance of me." Even the apostles needed a memento. It's almost holy. The need. To remember.

The Policeman starts off.

> Wait! It's not just me collecting. It's not sad. And it's not kinky. It's personal. Me and Marilyn.

Policeman: Personal?

Scout: Real personal.

Hollywood Premieres

Marilyn in a spot.

Marilyn: A Hollywood premiere is like the end of the world: when all of the stars in the expanding galaxy change direction, rush to the centre of the universe — otherwise known as Grauman's Chinese Theatre — and collide in a dense constellation leaving behind them nothing but gas. I carry a tiny black handbag, containing a delicate silver flask filled with expensive Scotch. I get a new gown covered with more sequins than the Sumerian zodiac has stars —

Scout: *Interrupting.* You sure know a lot of big words.

Marilyn: I never finished high school. I feel that my mind is beginning to atrophy. So I read science textbooks to improve my mental acuity.

Marilyn puts a pill in her mouth and washes it down with a glass of water.

I'd love to have some whiskey near me even now, just a titch, for running my lines. But I'm not supposed to have whiskey with these damn pills. Thanks to you and your defective bike.

Scout: Sorry about that.

Marilyn: You'll just have to make it up to me. *Chewing her lip.* I don't see how it can be such a big deal. I asked one of the boys to run downstairs and get me some, but he says Otto — Otto's the director — Otto gave the bell staff strict instructions that I'm not to touch the stuff. How old are you?

Scout: Seventeen.

Marilyn: I wish you were. I'd send you down to the bar for me. How old are you really? You can tell me.

Scout: Fifteen.

Marilyn: You can't be.

Scout: Am too.

Marilyn: A fifteen-year-old has chest hair.

Scout: I've got one.

Marilyn: Let's see.

Scout pulls up his shirt. He searches for a chest hair.

    Take it off.

Preoccupied with searching for his missing chest hair, Scout doesn't think to be embarrassed. He removes his shirt. He finds it.

Scout: There.

Marilyn: Where?

Scout: *Pointing.* Right here.

Marilyn: I can't see it.

Scout: It's blond. It's hard to see.

Marilyn moves closer.

Marilyn: Oh, there it is.

She touches his chest hair, over his heart, with her fingertip. The lights suddenly change. Marilyn freezes.

Scout: The first time she ever touched me it was like a surge of electricity. Not a shock. More like … an electromagnetic pulse. Marilyn? Can you hear me? I'll tell you a secret, Marilyn: I've been practicing. Trying to learn to control time. If I close my eyes and concentrate then I can slip in between the seconds. I can make time stop. Look: we can stay here as long as we choose.

Scout closes his eyes, blissfully. He sways. Marilyn is alive in the moment too — still, but not frozen. He opens his eyes and gazes at her.

He smiles.

See?

Lights change. The scene resumes. Marilyn rubs her hand across his chest.

Marilyn: Mmmm…. You are a big boy. I'll bet a big boy like you knows where a body can get a little splash of whiskey around here. Don't you?

Scout Steals a Drink

Mom is sitting in her chair, her bottle at her feet. She is barely conscious, but she manages to lock eyes with Scout. He looks at her for a moment. He crosses and grabs the bottle. He exits with it. Mom stirs.

Mom: What's the difference?

The Secret Cave and Basin

The Cave and Basin Hot Springs. It's warm and moist. Water drips and echoes. Marilyn and Scout enter quietly, almost reverently. Marilyn has the bottle, which she sips from often.

Marilyn: It smells … I don't know what. It reminds me of something … Oooh, the air it's … moist. It's like being by the ocean. Humid. The air's so dry in the mountains, I feel like my skin is cracking apart in the sun. But this … it's glorious. I can feel my skin healing. See?

She holds out her arm. Scout touches it.

Scout: It's soft.

Marilyn checks the water.

Marilyn: It's warm!

Scout: The water goes down through the cracks, so slowly you don't even notice. Down, down, down to the heart. And down there, at the heart, there's so much pressure that it gets really hot, and it builds up pressure, until it explodes in a big spray of scalding water.

Marilyn steps back startled.

Marilyn: Oh!

She bumps against Scout. He holds her gently.

Scout: But sometimes, if there isn't the pressure — then it's gentle. And beneficial. And that's how we get hot springs, like this.

Marilyn: How do you know all that?

Scout: It was my Science Fair project last year. The Indians thought the smelly water could cure them. Maybe it was all in their minds. But maybe, just maybe, it really does cure people.

Marilyn: Then, let's get in. Let's cure ourselves.

Scout: We didn't bring swimsuits.

Marilyn: So?

Marilyn starts taking her clothes off. Scout looks away.

Marilyn: What's the matter? Are you shy?

Scout: You're changing.

Marilyn: So? Haven't you ever seen a naked woman before?

Scout: No.

Marilyn: Not even your mother?

Scout: ... No.

Marilyn: Sure you have. Doesn't every little boy sneak a peek when their mother's changing her clothes?

Scout: No.

Marilyn: Well, then, sneak a peek.

Marilyn stands naked. Scout peeks, then looks away.

Is that it? Don't you want to take a longer look?

Scout looks again. Silence. Marilyn gets into the water. She stares at him.

Take your clothes off.

Scout: I'd best keep an eye out ...

Marilyn: I don't want to be in here all alone.

Scout: ... in case anyone comes ...

Marilyn: Take your clothes off.

Scout stares at her. He takes his clothes off.

Get in.

Scout enters the pool.

Come closer. Closer. Have you ever brought anyone else here?

Scout: I come with Bobby sometimes.

Marilyn: Ever brought one of the girls from town?

Scout: No.

Marilyn: So I'm your first?

Scout: Uh-huh.

Marilyn: Ooooh. It's so warm. It gets in your bones.

Scout: Uh-huh.

Marilyn begins to sing softly to herself the same lullaby that Mom sang earlier on the porch. Scout joins in. They laugh.

Where'd you learn that song?

Marilyn: I don't remember.

Pause. They stare at each other. Marilyn inhales deeply.

Epsom salts.

Scout: Huh?

Marilyn: That's what the smell reminds me of. Once, when I was
about your age, I was living in a foster home and they had
Epsom salts under the sink. I put them in my bath. I must
have put in too much, it was so salty. The husband came
in. Said he thought the pipes burst, it smelled so bad. He
stayed. Dipped his hand in the water to make sure it wasn't
too hot. He taught me things. I wasn't sure I wanted to
learn them, but... *Pause.* It's different for boys, isn't it?

Scout: Which?

Marilyn: Learning things. Boys like to learn things, don't they?

Scout: I'm not real good in school ...

Marilyn: I'm not talking about school.

*Marilyn reaches out and touches his penis, under the water. Scout closes
his eyes. Lights. While he speaks, he and Marilyn make love, gently,
in the water.*

Scout: This is the moment I wish I could stop. I keep trying,
but ... I don't get here very often and whenever I do, it
goes by so fast. *To Marilyn.* It only lasts a few minutes,
from the time you touch my Little Fellow until the time
we leave the Cave for fear of getting caught. I always want
it to last just a little longer. I try to think of something else.
I think of 1962 and the policeman. I think of the phone
call. I even try to think of Mom on the porch ... but ...
every time my Little Fellow with a mind of his own ...
realizes he has found his ... One ... And ... Only.

*Marilyn smiles and kisses him. They get out of the pool furtively, dressing
quickly, stealing quick, childish glances at each other as he speaks.*

Maybe I should give up and just be thankful. After all the
awful times that I have to visit over and over, for every late
night on the porch with Mom, for every time the policeman
stops me, I get to be here, with you — My One and Only.
I guess it makes reliving time in atomic order worth it.

They have finished dressing.

Marilyn: See you again?

Scout: Again. And again. And again.

They go separate ways, eyeing each other like young lovers.

On the Set

Scout is digging. Marilyn enters distractedly, crossing the stage. She doesn't see Scout.

Scout: Hi, Marilyn.

Marilyn: Oh! Scout. What are you doing?

Scout: I've got a job on the set.

Marilyn: *Nervously.* A job?

Scout: They've got me digging a ditch. More like a hole, really. For you.

Marilyn: For me?

Scout: I guess. For the movie anyway. How's your ankle?

Marilyn: Fine. Well, sore. I'm still taking the pills, just so I can walk on it.

Scout: Oh. Sorry about that. I guess I'll just have to make it up to you. Want me to run lines with you?

Marilyn: *Lying.* Uh … Otto doesn't want me learning any more lines. He says they sound practiced. Stilted. I'm just supposed to "be" in the moment.

Scout: Oh. Well, maybe I can help you "be."

Marilyn: I've got to go.

Marilyn starts off.

Scout: Miss Monroe?

Marilyn stops.

Did I do something wrong?

Marilyn: What? No.

Scout: Then why are you …?

Marilyn: Scout, you didn't do anything wrong. There's nothing wrong with sex. Sex is a natural thing, and what
could be wrong with a natural thing? It's something two
people do when they like each other. Don't ever think
you did anything wrong. OK?

She smiles at him gently.

You're a very sweet boy.

Marilyn exits. Scout is alone.

Scout: But a boy.

Atom Bomb

*Scout stands on the front porch, holding the pocket watch. Laughter
from inside the house, from both a man and a woman. Scout looks
around, confused about where and when he is.*

Scout: I'm a boy … eight years old … It's 1945 and I'm on
the porch with Mom. Mom? Mom? Mom!

Mom emerges from the house, unkempt.

Mom: Scout, shh, shh, you'll wake up the whole
neighbourhood.

Scout: Mom, I'm bored.

Mom: Now, what did we just say, Scout? Mommy and Daddy
need to be alone for a little while.

Daddy: *Offstage.* Hey! Flo!

Mom: Just a minute, sweetie. Now what did Daddy say about
that watch?

Scout: He said I should hang onto it. He said I should sit out here and not go inside. And he said that I could keep the watch.

Mom: *Smiling.* He did not say you could keep it, you little scamp.

Scout: He said I could hold onto the watch.

Mom: Not forever. Just until Daddy comes back out. And how long did Daddy say that would be?

Scout: Until the little hand is at the ...

Mom: Yes? Until the little hand is at the what?

Scout: Until the little hand is at the ten.

Daddy: *Offstage.* Flo! What's the holdup?

Mom: That's right, Scout. When the little hand reaches the ten, then you can knock on the door.

Scout: OK.

Mom exits. Scout sits on the porch, bored. He tosses the watch in the air a few times.

I didn't know it, but a bomb was dropping right about then. At 9:15, in Tokyo time, they dropped the first atom bomb. I saw pictures in *Life* magazine. There was the crystal-clear shape of a man burnt into the wall by the force of the blast, his hands trying to hide his face, kind of. In Honolulu, stoplights went crazy. In San Francisco, radios emitted nothing but static. And in a small town nestled in the Rocky Mountains ... Right now, the electromagnetic pulse from the very first atomic bomb is changing everything. We will never think of time the same way again. Ever.

Scout looks up into the sky, expectantly.

In Honolulu, in San Francisco, and in a small town in the Rocky Mountains, it's all the same time...

Tense pause.

Here it comes ...

A flash of bright white light illuminates the sky, accompanied by the sound of wind.

Daddy: Oh baby! Hallelujah!

Mom: *Offstage.* Oh baby ... It's like you make the earth move.

Scout gasps, even though he's seen it a thousand times before. He drops the watch in surprise. Scout bends down to pick up the watch.

Scout: It's broke. I think ... That's it! That's why time is so screwed up for me. Because ... of the bomb, because the pulse — the electromagnetic pulse ... atomic time is all crazy and out of step with itself, like this watch that couldn't start up proper again. That's why sometimes I skip forwards, sometimes back. I'm like this watch. But I nearly forgot ... every time, I nearly forget... I've got a secret ... I've been practicing. I figure, if I can squeeze in between those seconds, then maybe things can be —

What Are You Up To Tonight?

The phone rings many times. Scout goes to the phone.

Scout: Hello?

Marilyn: Scout?

Scout: Marilyn?

Marilyn: Scout, sweetie, I'm so sorry about the other day. I was so distracted .... the film and all ... You're not mad at me, are you?

Scout: No.

Marilyn: Scout, sweetie, do you think you can ... What are you up to tonight?

Scout: *Almost inaudible.* Nothing.

Marilyn: Are you there, Scout?

Scout: *Whispering.* I'm here, Marilyn. I don't want my Mom to hear.

Marilyn: *Whispering.* Why don't you come visit me, Scout? *Pause— then, whispering.* Otto's cut me off again, Scout.

Blackmail

Marilyn starts to take a sip. But her glass is empty. Scout is watching her. He holds up the bottle and waves it in the air. She changes gears suddenly, and slinks over to him. Scout holds the bottle aside. She put her arms around him. She kisses him full on the mouth. He pours her a glass.

Beauty Bazoombas

Scout is digging with a shovel. The shovel scrapes the ground, regularly scooping out dirt and piling it next to him. A **Townie** *enters and stares him.*

Townie: Aren't you done yet?

Scout: No.

Townie: Better hurry up, Scout. They want that done by tomorrow. First light. If you're still diggin' when all them people are sittin' on their asses paid to do nuthin', there'll be hell to pay.

Scout: I'm going as fast as I can, Mr. Palmer.

The Townie sits down to catch his breath.

Townie: Ah, they're still shootin' that river thing. They'll be hours yet. What was that Marilyn Monroe doin' up here all alone with you?

Scout: Nuthin'.

Townie: Nuthin', huh? I had to whistle for her half a dozen times before she came down the hill for the shoot. Did you get a look at the big ones on that little girl?

Scout: No.

Townie: I did.

Scout stops shoveling.

You should see her down there. They got her on the falls, on that raft. No pretend there; the water's rushin' over the sides with that current so strong even a grown man would be runnin' the risk of bein' swept away, let alone a little slip of a thing like her. I told that German director guy he should put some sorta safety rope 'round her, but that director, he says, "It's all about zee fear in her eyes." I think he was trying to show off for all those photographers who came up from Hollywood today. Shouldn't've opened my big mouth, he wouldn't've sent me up here. Anyhow, the point is, she's soaking wet, white blouse clinging to them beauty bazoombas, red nips big as cherry tomatoes, standin' at attention out to here. Might as well be starkers.

Scout grips his shovel.

All them photographers were crowded as close to the shore as they can without bein' in the shot, just so they can get a good picture. *He winks.* Tell the truth, I think she likes it. A big swell pulled her top down to her waist once. She didn't even pull it up until the scene was over. And get this — when they called out "cut," I swear — she was smilin' at me. *He chuckles.* Some little whore.

Scout leaps forward, with the shovel raised.

Scout: You shut up!

Townie: Scout! What's wrong with you?

Scout: She's not. Hear me?

Townie: What?

Scout: She's no whore.

Townie: Haven't you read the papers?

Scout takes a swing at the Townie. He misses, drops the shovel and takes off.

　　Crazy son of a bitch. Just like his mother.

Lights. The sound of the river can be heard in the darkness. It grows and swells, irresistibly, like the forces of passion itself. It builds until...

You Have to Share

A forest path. Scout prowls, waiting. Marilyn enters; Scout surprises her.

Scout: You don't give a fat rat's ass who sees your boobs! Just let your top fall down and show everybody your goods, don't you?

Marilyn: I was holding on for dear life. With both hands. I was soaking wet and that stupid wig — What did you want me to do? Let go? Protect my modesty and get swept downriver?

Scout: They all saw! The whole town!

Marilyn: Right into the rapids, both hands holding up that stupid top, never mind my head banging against the rocks.

Scout: You liked it.

Marilyn: *Sarcastically, angrily.* I loved it. I love being stuck on a raft in a freezing cold river for five hours. I love hypothermia. I get hot when creepy old men leer at my boobs while I'm fighting for my life.

Scout: Then why'd you do it for?

Marilyn: Because I was told to.

Scout: You're the star.

Marilyn: And the star does as she's told. You have to dig
a ditch. I have to get soaking wet to titillate America.

Scout: Those photographers! Mr. Palmer told me they were
taking pictures.

Marilyn: I'm in fucking Canada! And right this second Betty
Grable or Diana Dors, or — or — or some other blonde is
down there in Los Angeles doing "the business." But do
you want to know where I'm going to be tomorrow? I'm
going to be back in business. Because those pictures are
going to be in every living room in America.

Scout: So! It was on purpose.

Marilyn: My body is my business. If it generates a little interest,
a little "business," then that's just part of the job. *Suddenly
exhausted.* It isn't easy. You have to be two people at once.
They turn the camera on, and you have be Marilyn Monroe,
but with real feelings at the same time. It drives you nuts.
But the illusion of my glamour is important to the business.
And so I pretend to a certain reputation.

Scout: Pretend?

Marilyn opens her coat, suddenly seductive.

Marilyn: They're just boobs. Inflated globes. Rich with blood
and milk.

Scout: They're mine.

Marilyn takes him inside and holds him.

Marilyn: You have to share, honey. I know it's hard. But you have
to share.

She kisses him.

Scout: *Whispering.* Am I your only one?

Marilyn breaks away with a frustrated sigh.

Marilyn: Ahh! Why do you always have to go and ruin it?

Scout: Am I your One and Only?

Marilyn: Stop talking like that.

Scout: Am I?

Marilyn: I don't belong to one person. I belong to the world.
And the world belongs to me.

Scout: So ... that's it then ...

Marilyn: No ... Scout, I didn't mean — You don't even know
when you're in love.

Scout: Then tell me: How do you know when you fall in love?

Marilyn throws up her arms and starts to walk away.

How do you know? Tell me!

Marilyn turns.

Marilyn: *Frankly.* I don't know.

Stuck in the Gate

*Scout sits in a chair, just as he did at the top of the show. He is
watching a movie in a movie theatre. The light plays across his face,
flickering. The sound of an old-fashioned film projector and muffled
dialogue from a film can be heard indistinctly.*

*The film gets caught in the gate, skipping like a record. We hear the
same line, Marilyn's voice, over and over again.*

*The Policeman enters, shining his flashlight; he might look like an
usher, or a night watchman. A tear stains Scout's cheek. He holds his
head in his hands. The Policeman shines the light in Scout's face.*

Love Sick

Scout sits up.

Policeman: Personal, was it?

Scout: She was my One And Only.

Policeman: She was a lot of people's one and only.

Scout: You take that back.

Policeman: Just calm down there, son.

Scout: I'm telling you, it was —

Policeman: Yeah, yeah, I know. It was "personal."

Scout: It was! Marilyn and I — in Banff — in 1953 — she was shooting *River of No Return* and we ... she was ... she was my One and Only.

Policeman: Your one ...? Oh, you mean ... *personal.*

Scout nods.

Marilyn Monroe, huh? Sheesh. You must have been pretty young.

Scout: What do you know.

Policeman: I know. Believe me, I know. Mitzi-Mitzi. Stripper. Blonde, beautiful. I stopped her on the side of the road, same as you. I guess she figured I was less trouble than the ticket. She was my first, even though I was twenty-one. She liked that — being my first. She said it made her feel like she could "start over." And me, well, I was just glad to be starting. I got all sorts of ideas into my head. A house with a little yard, white picket fence, the whole works ... stupid ideas. Then one day, out of the blue, she wouldn't answer the phone, wouldn't talk to me. The only way I could see her was if I went and watched her dance... And I did ... I watched her dance, night after night until it got me right here — *Pounds his chest, pauses, frowns.* — or here — *Rubs his stomach, frowns.* — kinda both. Like I had an ache in the stomach, and indigestion at the same time. If you know what I mean.

Scout: Yeah. I do.

Policeman: I got a memento of my own.

The Policeman reaches inside his pocket, hesitates; then looks at Scout and decides to share with him after all. He pulls two small red disks out of his pocket and shows them to Scout, shamefaced. Scout looks at them blankly.

Scout: What are those?

Policeman: Pasties. The kind strippers wear.

The Policeman puts them over his chest, where his nipples might be. He dances, a little too sensuously.

> I wanted something to … well, like you said, a memento … We used to …

Lost in thought for a moment he holds them out in front of him, one on each side. He fondles the ends of the pasties and is about to … when he pulls back.

> You want to know what I think, Scout? I think you're sick. Lovesick. Or sick of love, which amounts to the same thing.

Scout: She was my One And Only.

Silence.

Policeman: Have you ever slept with anybody *but* Marilyn Monroe, Scout? *Long silence.* Like the Virgin Mary. Are you going to want to kiss some carpenter after you've kissed God? *Even longer silence.* There's a difference between being in love and being lovesick. You do know that, don't you, Scout? We folk who've been made lovesick, we don't know any other kind, do we? I'll tell you why you drove a couple thousand miles. You needed to get rid of that ache in your stomach. You thought maybe if you had something of hers, then you'd have something to hang onto. But lemme tell you something …

He holds up the pasties.

I've carried these things in my uniform every shift for God knows how many years, I've got three kids, and still, when I wake up in the middle of the night I'm not thinking about their mother. If you hang onto it now, you ain't never gonna be able to get rid of it. Look.

The Policeman weighs the pasties in his hands, like they were lead bullets. He throws them with all of his might into the audience. But it is like throwing feathers — or dreams — they are too insubstantial to catch the wind and leave him. They flutter to earth at his feet. He stares at where they fell. Pause.

See?

They stare at the pasties.

Seems to me like you're stuck, Scout. Seems to me your memento is a part of it. Is that about right?

Scout: That's about right.

A long silence. The Policeman pulls the car keys from his pocket.

Policeman: Might as well get it over with.

He starts off towards the back of the car. Scout follows him, anxious.

Scout: Wait — Don't make me —

Policeman: Don't give me that hangdog look. I'll tell you what I'll do — I'll give you a choice — if you give me your memento, I'll knock fifty miles an hour off the speeding ticket. Fifty miles an hour. You give me any more trouble — and I'll give you something else.

Scout: Don't make me.

The Policeman tosses the keys in the air and deftly catches them in his hand.

Policeman: You've got a choice, Scout.

The Policeman opens the trunk.

Phone Ringing (2)

A phone rings in the black. Several times. Scout answers with great trepidation.

Scout: Hello?

Marilyn: *Tired, drugged.* Scout?

Scout: Marilyn?

Marilyn: Scout, is that you?

Pause.

Are you there, Scout?

Scout: I'm here, Marilyn.

Marilyn: You sound all grown up, Scout.

Scout: It's been ... a long time.

Marilyn: Why didn't you ever come visit me, Scout? Don't you
    miss me?

Scout: Where are you?

Marilyn: The City of Angels ... I'm so ... tired ... of all the
    bull — hic ... ooopsy. Shouldn't have had — hic —
    so much to drink ... not with all those ...

Pause.

Scout: Marilyn?

Marilyn: Scout ... there's something I never ... never told you ...

Pause.

Scout: What is it, Marilyn?

Silence.

Marilyn? Marilyn? Marilyn?

Scout sets down the phone.

Sometimes Back

Scout stares at the Policeman. The Policeman tosses the keys in the air and deftly catches them in his hand.

Policeman: You've got a choice, Scout.

Scout closes his eyes and concentrates.

Scout: *Chanting to himself.* … between the time it's running forward and the time it starts running back … squeeze in between those seconds … squeeze in between those seconds …

The Policeman opens the trunk.

Policeman: What the sweet Jesus is this?

Scout: Make it stop! … make it change.

The Policeman starts to move backwards, like a film moving in reverse. He retraces his blocking in reverse up to the point that he gets the license from Scout. The Policeman stands still, frozen, holding the license out in midair beside the car. Scout opens his eyes. When he does …

On the Side of Rocky Mountain (2)

Marilyn lies on the ground. Scout is shoveling. She props her head up on one arm.

Marilyn: Kinda sexy the way you sweat in the sun.

Scout: I stink.

Marilyn: It's kinda sexy.

Scout: What's sexy about sweat?

Marilyn: Reminds me. Of the times we sweat together.

Scout flips some dirt her way. She laughs. They smile together.

Leave that.

Scout: Can't. They want it done before first light tomorrow. How's your ankle?

Marilyn: Better. I'm still taking those pills.

Scout: Sorry about that.

Marilyn: You'll just have to make it up to me.

She smiles. Scout blushes. She stares up at the mountain.

Our mountain. It's got a … special place in my heart. Like it knows who I am. Like it's been waiting its whole life for me to come here and make my movie. It'd be a shame to leave it and never see it again. Someday, I want to be buried here. On the side of Rocky Mountain. Come here.

Scout: Can't.

Marilyn unbuttons her blouse. Scout doesn't notice until she brings it to his attention.

Marilyn: I'll make it worth your while.

Scout sees her. He starts towards her, as if to make love to her. He stops himself, suddenly aware.

Scout: I can't.

Marilyn: *Pouting.* Why not?

Scout: I can't do this again.

Marilyn: It was only this morning. I think you're a better lover than you know.

Scout: Not again.

Marilyn: *Reaching for his belt.* I'll help.

Scout: You're going to die.

Marilyn: Don't say that.

Scout: It's true.

Marilyn: We all have to die sometime, Scout —

Scout: I know when. I do. I've been there.

Marilyn: Now you're being silly.

Scout: I wish I could change things from the way they are to the way I want them to be. I know what's going to happen, but I get so caught up in things and then before I know it, it's happening again, the exact same way as before.

Pause. Marilyn laughs uncomfortably.

I'm telling you. I've been here before.

Marilyn: We all get déjà vu sometimes.

Scout: We haven't got much time. They'll be ready for you in a second.

Marilyn peers over his shoulder and stands on tiptoe.

Marilyn: How can you tell? I can't see anything from here.

Scout: Mr. Palmer's going to whistle for you in a second. Then he's going to take you down to the river ... then he's going to come back and tell me what happened.

Marilyn: He is, is he?

Scout: He's been sent up here to get you, because he's always shooting off his mouth. But he's too lazy to climb the hill; that's why he whistles.

Pause. They wait. A whistle.

See?

Marilyn: You saw him. You must have.

Scout: Am I your One and Only?

Marilyn: Oh, for Christ's sake.

Another whistle.

Scout: You never answer the question. All the times I ever ask it. I don't care what the answer is. I just need to know how you feel —

Marilyn: Scout, do you have to ask?

Scout: How you really feel? Without all the sex?

Marilyn: Scout ...

Scout: Tell me now. Before it's too late.

Another whistle.

Marilyn: I've got to go.

Scout: You die.

Marilyn: Scout!

Scout: You die before you can tell me. And I do what you asked me to. About this mountain.

Marilyn: That's a horrible thing to say.

Scout: But if we can both remember — at the same time — then maybe it can be different. You have to promise me, the next time we're together — promise me you'll try to make a different choice.

Marilyn: I ... I have to go.

Marilyn goes. Scout shouts after her.

Scout: Try! Promise? Just try!

Bottle Dance

Scout searches for the bottle. He sees Mom standing with it, watching him. She waves the bottle in the air. He crosses to her and they stare at one another. He reaches for it. She holds the bottle aside. They stare. She shrugs and hands it to him.

The Talk

Marilyn stands wearing her coat, scarf, and glasses, with suitcases piled beside her, fidgeting. She takes her glasses off and wipes her eyes — and we realize that she hasn't been fidgeting, she's been crying. Scout enters.

Marilyn: Did you bring it?

Scout holds up a bottle. Marilyn holds out her hand, but Scout refuses to bring it to her. Marilyn sighs and limps towards him. She twists her ankle on the walk.

Ow!

She snatches the bottle from him.

You said you'd bring it by six.

Scout: I got held up.

Marilyn: I'll say.

Marilyn shakes a few pills into her hand and swallows them.

Scout: Are you sure you should —

Marilyn: What?

Scout: I don't think you're supposed to take so many of those —

Marilyn: Maybe I wouldn't need to if someone hadn't given me a defective bike.

Scout: What am I supposed to do to make it up to you?

Marilyn drops some pills on the ground.

Marilyn: Shit!

She gets down on her hands and knees and tries to retrieve the pills before they roll away. She stops, defeated, and hangs her head, still on her knees.

What's the difference?

Scout: You sound like my mother.

Marilyn: *Exploding, irrational.* I'm not going to be a mother. I'm not.

Scout: What?

Marilyn: I'm going away for a few days, Scout. I'm going to have a little operation. It's a simple procedure. I've had it before. When I was in foster care, after the ... Epsom salts.

Scout: Are you sick?

Marilyn: I'm having an abortion, Scout.

Pause.

Scout: What's an abortion?

Marilyn: Oh, Scout ... *Under her breath.* Oh my God, what have I done? *To Scout.* Scout, darling ... I'm pregnant.

Scout: Oh. *Pause.* I know I'm not supposed to, not until after the wedding, but I think I should stay at your house. It'll be better, what with the baby coming and all.

Marilyn: Are you having me on ...?

Scout: Do you have an apartment or a house? A little yard would be better, for the baby, wouldn't it?

Marilyn: There's not going to be a baby! I'm taking the train into the city, and I'm going to have an operation to get rid of the baby. It's not going to be born.

Scout: Oh.

Marilyn: And then I'm coming back here just for the last few days of shooting, and then ... and then the film is going to be over, Scout.

Scout: Over?

Marilyn: Yes. Over. All things come to an end. Jesus, you're not even old enough to drive me to the station.

Scout: You were old enough.

Marilyn: What?

Scout: You were married when you were my age. You said.
So ... we could ... couldn't we?

Marilyn: Scout, that's ... it's different for boys. Boys should
marry someone ... their own age.

Scout: Why?

Marilyn: They just should.

Scout: I don't want to marry someone else, I want —

Marilyn: I know what you want, Scout ... but you can't have it,
so you might as well not want it. Sometimes we don't have
a choice —

The penny drops for Scout.

Scout: Yes. Yes, we do. You do. Do you remember when we
were on our mountain? I told you, you can make a
different choice? This time we're going to do it different
— Marilyn, try to remember — try to do it different
this time.

The train whistle goes.

Marilyn: I guess that's my train.

Scout: Let's try to do it different this time. Can you hear me,
Marilyn?

Marilyn: Don't say that, Scout. Maybe we will see each other
someday.

*She is clearly hearing something different come out of Scout's mouth
than we are.*

Scout: You can hear me, I know you can. I'm not saying the
same thing I always I say. I'm saying something different.

Marilyn: Well, I might want to see you again.

Scout: Listen. Listen to me. I'm saying something different. You can too.

Marilyn: Don't say you hate me, Scout. I don't know if I could bear that.

Scout: We can change things from the way they really happened to the way we want them to be. We can have that other life. You and me, and the house and the baby ... we'll be together and you'll stop drinking and you won't die from those pills. And you'll live. With me. On the side of our mountain.

She slaps him.

Marilyn: Don't you ever, ever call me a whore.

The train whistle again.

My body might be my business, but no one calls me a whore. No one.

Marilyn grabs her things and crosses to the door.

Scout: We have a choice.

Marilyn: I don't care if I ever see you again as long as I live either.

Scout: We have a choice!

Marilyn is gone. The train whistles in the distance like a mournful howl.

Old Lady Blackbird

Mom is waiting on the porch. Scout slowly goes and gets his cup. He sits down and holds it out to Mom. She pours him a glass.

Mom: You gonna keep your old Mom company for a while?

Scout: For a while.

Mom tousles Scout's hair. She draws his head into her lap and continues stroking his hair gently. She sings her favourite lullaby softly, now the third time we've heard it.

Silence.

Scout: The earth moved, Mom.

Mom: What's that mean, the earth moved?

Scout: What's the difference?

Mom's hand gradually moves from his hair down his body.

Mom ...

Mom: A lot of people can make the earth move.

Silence. Mom gives Scout a sloppy, creepy kiss. Scout doesn't stop her. Pause. Then:

What's in the trunk, Scout?

Scout: What did you say?

Mom: I'm not going to show you my boobs for a nickel.

Scout: Mom ...?

Marilyn emerges from the shadows.

Marilyn: What would you say if your old Mom told you she'd take you to see Marilyn Monroe?

Scout: Marilyn ...?

Mom: I play Kay, the most beautiful woman in the whole wild west, but also, the loneliest.

Scout: Who are you?

The Policeman takes back the license and looks at it. The Policeman starts moving forward again, without dialogue, repeating his movements in fast motion.

No ... No ...

Marilyn: Do you want to step out of the car please, son?

Mom: I'll just bet you got a few evil spirits, don't you, Scout?

Scout: Stop it.

Mom: Haven't you ever seen a naked woman before? Not even your mother?

Marilyn: Red nipples big as cherry tomatoes, standing at attention out to here. Might as well be starkers.

Mom: Are you an orphan? I can spot an orphan right away.

Scout: Just stop it.

Scout holds his ears. He sinks to the floor.

Mom: Oh baby! Hello Daddy!

Marilyn: Boys like to learn things, don't they?

Mom: I'll bet a big boy like you knows where a body can get a little splash of whiskey around here.

Marilyn: Marilyn Monroe — she took all of the Warner brothers at the same time … all four of 'em up the poop chute.

Mom: They dropped the bomb on Japan right about then.

The Policeman stops upstage, beside the car. He pulls the car keys from his pocket. He tosses the keys in the air and deftly catches them in his hand.

Policeman: You've got a choice, Scout.

Marilyn: Scout? Scout? Scout?

Scout looks up. Marilyn takes him by the hand and helps him to his feet. She gently places the shovel into his hands.

Someday, I want to be buried here. On the side of Rocky Mountain.

Marilyn nods towards the Policeman. The Policeman opens the trunk.

Policeman: What the sweet Jesus is this?

Scout hits the Policeman with the shovel. He goes down.

Scout: I guess that'll teach me to watch my speed. There's a lot of cops between here and that mountain.

He looks in the trunk.

I'll be a minute, Marilyn.

Scout closes the trunk. He starts shoveling a hole for the Policeman, humming softly to himself.

On the Side of Rocky Mountain (3)

Marilyn lies on the ground. Scout is shoveling and singing. Marilyn props her head up on one arm.

Marilyn: Kinda sexy the way you sweat in the sun.

Scout: I stink.

Marilyn: It's kinda sexy.

Scout: What's sexy about sweat?

Marilyn: Reminds me. Of the times we sweat together.

Scout flips some dirt her way. She laughs. They smile together.

Leave that.

Scout: Can't. They want it done before first light tomorrow.

She stares up at the mountain.

Marilyn: Our mountain. It's got a … special place in my heart. Like it knows who I am. Like it's been waiting its whole life, for me to come here and make my movie. It would be a shame to leave it, and never see it again. Someday, I want to be buried here. On the side of Rocky Mountain. Come here.

Scout: Can't.

Marilyn unbuttons her blouse. Scout doesn't notice until she brings it to his attention.

Marilyn: I'll make it worth your while.

Scout sets down his shovel and leaps down beside her. They kiss passionately, inexpertly. Like children. They pause.

Scout: I can't bury you here. It's too shallow. The bears'll get you. Dig you up and eat you.

Marilyn: Better than being eaten by worms. *She shudders at the thought.* It's just a body. I don't care.

Scout: Then why do you care where you'll be buried?

Marilyn: For you. So you can come up here and stand by my grave and cry because I'm dead.

Scout: I can visit the graveyard.

Marilyn: Too easy. I want you to have to make an effort. *Pause.* Promise me.

Scout: What? That I'll leave you buried on some mountain where you'll get eaten by bears?

Marilyn: Promise?

Scout: Sure. I promise.

Scout resumes digging. A whistle is heard from offstage. Marilyn frowns. Scout notices.

What's the matter?

Marilyn: I just got the strangest sense of déjà vu.

Scout: And?

Marilyn: I don't know.

Scout waits, hopefully. The whistle again. Marilyn stands, still frowning, troubled by a half-remembered thought.

Scout: Marilyn? Is there something ...?

Marilyn is about to speak. Scout waits, afraid to even breathe. The whistle again.

Marilyn: I am buried here. Already. Aren't I?

Scout nods. Marilyn silently gathers her things and begins to head off, while Scout watches. She stops and turns.

Scout ...

Scout: Yes.

Marilyn: You're my ...

She catches herself. She looks at her feet.

Scout: It's okay, Marilyn. You don't have to —

Marilyn: You're very important to me. I don't think I've ever felt this way about anyone.

Marilyn smiles at him. She leaves. Scout stares after her. He shrugs.

Scout: *To himself.* Close enough.

Scout resumes digging. He begins to sing the theme music to himself softly. The shape of Marilyn is in the shadows. She joins him. They sing together, about how lost love is like a river; they sing about yearning; they sing until the lights fade ...

THE END

Ken Cameron is a Calgary-based playwright and all-around arts administrator. He is the author of more than fifteen plays, including *Harvest,* which premiered in a nearly sold-out run at Ontario's Blyth Festival in 2008. Ken is also the author of *My Morocco,* which toured Western Canada and was nominated for Outstanding New Play at Calgary's Betty Mitchell Awards; and *My One And Only,* which received an Honourable Mention in the Herman Voaden National Playwriting Competition, and was nominated for the Gwen Pharis Ringwood Award for playwriting and the Betty Mitchell Award for Outstanding New Play. Ken is the artistic director of the Magnetic North Theatre Festival, Canada's National Festival of Contemporary Canadian Theatre. With a mandate to showcase Canada's outstanding touring productions, Magnetic North is produced in Ottawa in odd-numbered years, and in a different Canadian city every other year. Ken lives in Calgary with his wife Rita Bozi.

KEN CAMERON PLAYOGRAPHY

Harvest
— Lunchbox Theatre, Calgary, March/April 2007, dir. Ian Prinsloo.
— Winner of the Enbridge playRites Award 2007.
— Blyth Festival, June/August 2008, dir. Ian Prinsloo.
— Port Stanley Summer Theatre, July/Aug 2009, dir. Beth Bruck.
— Victoria Playhouse, Petrolia and The Red Barn Theatre, Jackson's
  Point, Ontario, July/Aug, 2009, dir. Robert More.
— Shadow Theatre, Edmonton, October 2009, dir. John Hudson.

My Morocco
— Oh Solo Mio Festival, London, Ontario, April 2006, dir. Andy Curtis.
— Winnipeg Fringe Theatre Festival, July 2006.
— Saskatoon Fringe Theatre Festival, August 2006.
— Edmonton International Fringe Theatre Festival, August 2006.
— Ground Zero Theatre and One Yellow Rabbit, Calgary, April, 2007.

Dragonfly: Episode IV, Identity
(with Anita Miotti and David van Belle)
— Calgary Fringe Theatre Festival, August 2006, dir. Anita Miotti and
  David van Belle.
— Edmonton International Fringe Theatre Festival, August 2006.
— Big Secret Theatre, Theatre of the Living Statue, May 2007, dir.
  Ron Jenkins.

My One and Only
— Alberta Theatre Projects, playRites 2004, January 2004, dir. Gail
  Hanrahan.
— Nominated for Outstanding New Play at Calgary's Betty Mitchell
  Awards.
— Honourable Mention in the Herman Voaden National Playwriting
  Competition.
— Nominated for the Gwen Pharis Ringwood Award for Playwriting.
— Workshop West Theatre, Edmonton, April 2005, dir. Ron Jenkins.
— Produced as *Making Marilyn* by the Bridge Theatre Company,
  New York City, October 2005, dir. Robin A. Patterson.

Might As Well Live: The Words of Dorothy Parker
(adapted from Dorothy Parker, with Laura Parken)
— The Art Ranch, October 2003, dir. Gail Hanrahan.

Doppelganger
(based on a script by Simon Heath, with contributions from Bonnie
Bowman, Rita Bozi, Ron Chambers, Doug Curtis, Elyne Quan, and
Eugene Stickland)
— The Art Ranch, 2002, dir. Ken Cameron.
Stop Thinking!
— The Art Ranch, January 1999, dir. Ken Cameron.

Alien Love Connection
— Lunchbox Theatre, October 1997, dir. Kevin McKendrick.

The Climate: A Province in deKlein
(with Doug Curtis and Laura Parken)
— The Art Ranch, January 1997, dir. Ken Cameron and Laura Parken.

Black Tongue
— The Art Ranch, January 1996, dir. Ken Cameron.

Bloody Knuckles
— Players Theatre, Montreal, March 1992.
— Creations Etc., Montreal, 1992, dir. Sean Devine.
— Theatre in the Tent, University of Calgary, 1994, dir. Adam Leigh
  and Lester Fong.

Mrs. Talleyhouse
— Playwrights Workshop Montreal Write on the Edge Festival, March
  1992, dir. Sheldon Rosen.
— Garry Theatre, May 1995, dir. Kelly Daniels.